More
TEA SHOP WALKS
in
THE LAKE DISTRICT

Norman & June Buckley

Published by Sigma Leisure – an imprint of
Sigma Press, 1 South Oak Lane, Wilmslow, Cheshire SK9 6AR, England.

British Library Cataloguing in Publication Data
A CIP record for this book is available from the British Library.

ISBN: 1-85058-631-4

Typesetting and Design by: Sigma Press, Wilmslow, Cheshire.

Cover: Coniston Water from Brantwood (June Buckley)

Maps: Alan Bradley

Photographs: the authors

Printed by: MFP Design and Print

Disclaimer: the information in this book is given in good faith and is believed to be correct at the time of publication. No responsibility is accepted by either the author or publisher for errors or omissions, or for any loss or injury howsoever caused. Only you can judge your own fitness, competence and experience.

Preface

The production of a second volume of Lake District tea shop walks needs no apology. Although the area of the district is comparatively small, its pre-eminence as the finest and most popular walking area in England is well-earned. There is no lack of attractive and well varied routes waiting to be discovered by those who enjoy the combination of a modest circular walk with a recommended tea shop.

Similarly, the twenty tea shops included in 'Tea Shop Walks in the Lake District' (Sigma Press) have by no means exhausted the rich diversity of catering establishments qualifying for, and worthy of inclusion in, a 'tea shop' book. The popularity of the previous volumes in this series confirms that the formula works; the more generous 30 walks and tea shops included in this book should give at least as much pleasure as their predecessors.

The 'modest walks' average about five miles in length, with a range of two to nine miles. Unlike the author's 'Level Walks' series (SigmaLeisure), some hill climbs are included although most of the walks are at comparatively low level. Difficulties such as rock scrambling and sharp ridges are avoided. The presumption remains that many walkers, possibly including those with young families, want a clearly defined walk in attractive countryside, if possible with some features of particular interest incorporated, but without having to spend time and effort – and possible anguish! – on route finding. This presumption has been the guiding factor in writing the book.

It follows that a short but accurate assessment of the walk must be set out at the outset in each case so that judgement as to its suitability for any person(s) or occasion may be made very quickly. This assessment includes the length of the walk, the type of countryside, any hills or mountains climbed, any towns or villages visited, the condition of footpaths and/or lanes used and a recommendation for car parking.

The intention is that the walks will be circular and that the tea shop will, wherever feasible, be situated part way round the circuit. For obvious reasons such as limited car parking places, the refreshments have to be at the end of some walks. Footpaths and bridleways, keeping to established rights of way and 'permissive' paths, are always the first choice routes, using surfaced lanes and minor roads only when unavoidable. On higher ground, 'access land' carries a general permission for walkers. As usual in these books, parts of established continuous routes such as the Cumbria Way and the Allerdale Ramble are included.

In the Lake District it is hardly necessary to differentiate the 'best' areas for walking The whole district, including the fringes, has a great deal to offer. In the middle are the spectacular high mountains, girt by steep crags, tumbling scree and ice-carved valleys, with lakes such as Buttermere and Wastwater. In the lower reaches of the valleys and on the outer fringes the landscape is more gentle, but the rewards offered to walkers by the lakes and tarns and their wooded shores, the stone built villages and ancient farmsteads, are just as great.

The other essential ingredient of each walk is, of course, the availability of refreshment along the way. Assessment of the various 'tea shops' is always done carefully and the description is written so that everyone will know what to expect in the range of catering, from the basic pot of tea to quite sophisticated cooked food. As ever, efforts are made to diversify and the term 'tea shop' can and does include a rich mixture of premises, the sampling of which is an important part of the pleasure awaiting readers of this book. Inevitably, some of the tea shops open only during the main holiday season and at other busy times such as Bank Holidays, whilst others restrict winter opening to weekends. Every effort has been made to give accurate information on opening dates and hours, but it has to be accepted that changes are very often made at short notice, sometimes even depending on the weather on a particular day. Telephone numbers are given in all cases for up to the minute advice.

To complement the route of the walk and the teashop recommendation, a concise 'About the Area' section comments on towns, villages, visitor attractions and interesting features encountered on the walk.

Although these walks are not generally strenuous, do remember that the Lake District is predominantly mountain country, subject to sudden changes in the weather, and that extra clothing, including waterproofs, and emergency food should always be carried. Even on the easiest walk in the district, most walkers will find that there is no real alternative to wearing proper boots, waterproof and with shaped, thick, semi-rigid soles. Swamps are common and footpaths rapidly become impromptu watercourses in wet weather. Stony ground soon becomes painful to the feet through soles without thickness or rigidity.

It has always been true to say that, however good the route description and associated sketch plan, the use of a detailed map such as those produced to the scale of 1: 25,000 by the Ordnance Survey, will add interest for the walker who is prepared to spend a little time on its study. In countryside as rich and varied as the Lake District, this added interest is probably greater than anywhere else in the country. Appropriate recommendations are, therefore, made.

Acknowledgement

The authors wish to express their appreciation of the assistance and companionship of John and Ann Ainley-Walker who, together with the unfailingly enthusiastic Jemma and Jinty, have been involved in many of the walks in this book.

Norman & June Buckley

Publisher's Note

Unlike many guidebooks that feature cafés or restaurants,
we do not accept payment by any establishment for
inclusion in our books. Selection is purely on merit and
for convenience on a particular walking route. There may be
many other tea shops that are equally worth calling on
– please send in your suggestions!

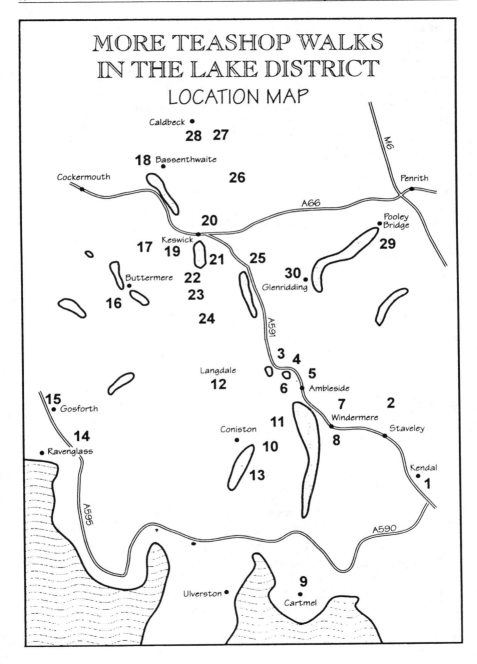

MORE TEASHOP WALKS IN THE LAKE DISTRICT
LOCATION MAP

Contents

Introduction

There are many comprehensive descriptions of the history of the Lake District, usually starting with the complex geological circumstances which have given the area its basic shape and continuing with the elemental forces which have affected that basic shape over the subsequent millions of years. The first 'tea shop' book (*Tea Shop Walks in The Lake District*, by Jean Patefield, also published by Sigma Leisure) sets out this history at some length, emphasising the importance of the last ice age, which finally retreated only 10,000 or so years ago, to the landscape which we see today.

After all, for the great majority of visitors to the district it is what we see on the surface today which is paramount, resulting from the steady colonisation by plants, shrubs and trees as the ice retreated and, perhaps most important factor of all, the effect of the arrival of man, the hunter, the farmer, the miner, the quarryman, the charcoal burner, the builder, the incoming resident and, latterly, the tourist.

Had man not arrived we must presume that the area would still be almost totally covered by forest, spare and windswept on the higher fell sides, swampy and alder dominated in the valley bottoms. So, what we now see is by no means a 'natural' landscape; most of it is a farming landscape, even the fell tops being modified by sheep grazing and the fell sides showing the evidence of attempts to take in and improve ever more land at times when population increase put pressure on farming output and the valley bottoms had long been cleared of the forest cover. It is a sobering thought that today's Lakeland farming, on small areas of comparatively difficult, unproductive, land is, of necessity, heavily subsidised from public funds, be it the much maligned Common Agricultural Policy of the European Union or a national predecessor. Any reform which rationalised farming by concentrating production on the richer lands of the south and the midlands or, indeed, in other countries of the Union, where any particular activity could be profitable or at least self-supporting, would result in the cessation of Lake District farming. The return to a 'natural' landscape would commence at once and the result would probably, to most people, be far less attractive than the wonderful blend of natural and man-made which we enjoy today.

In some parts, the effects of industry outweigh those attributable to farming; the quarrying of Tilberthwaite and the post-mining dere-

liction of Coppermines Valley, Coniston are major landscape ele-
ments. The need for charcoal to fuel small scale smelting,
gunpowder production and other rural industries also had its effect
on the original woodland, although the need for a renewable re-
source resulted in the development of coppicing and management
of the trees rather than clearance.

Despite the appearance of permanence, landscape evolution is inevitably a dynamic process. An area such as Lakeland can never be
'frozen' at a particular point in time however much it might be ad-
mired as it is. This was never more true than at the present time,
when the effects of mass tourism are impacting on a small and vul-
nerable area. More disposable income, independent mobility resulting from almost universal motor car ownership and more spare time
all combine to bring more visitors. The motor car in particular
causes intense problems as both the access roads to the district and
the minor roads within the district are inadequate at many peak periods. At these times there are also nothing like enough car-parking
spaces. To attempt to provide for these perceived needs and for
those who, for example, want to bring power boats for fast, noisy,
water sports, would accelerate change to the landscape at a rate far
faster than anything known since man first arrived on the scene and
commenced felling trees with stone axes. Apart from the concern
about the pace of change, the main consideration has to be whether
or not that change could be any way beneficial to the landscape and
to its enjoyment by the great majority of residents and visitors. The
answer, at least from those who will be spending time walking in
this sublime countryside, has to be a resounding 'no'.

During the present century it has become ever more obvious that
the public interest, yours and mine, in these matters cannot be protected unless laws are passed and publicly appointed bodies are em-
powered to enforce them on our behalf. Hence town and country
planning authorities. Special protection has been given to the Lake
District and several other areas of outstanding importance by creat-
ing a 'National Park', where the rules on land development and use
are more strict than throughout the rest of the country and are en-
forced by the Park Authority itself. Despite this relatively strong
planning control situation, there are almost constant pressures from
would-be developers of holiday villages, estates of 'desirable resi-
dences', caravan sites, and others whose motivation is profit rather
than the preservation of the landscape. The planning authority is of-

ten in difficulty in resisting these pressures and, too often, loopholes are found whereby some virtually irrevocable change takes place.

However, in conclusion, let us give thanks for National Parks, for the National Trust which owns a large proportion of the Lake District, for Forest Enterprises, which is now 'walker-friendly' and for those enlightened landowners who, over the years, have negotiated accesses for walkers and some who have, like Beatrix Potter, bequeathed so much to the National Trust for enjoyment by the public in perpetuity. In giving thanks, as responsible walkers let us not forget our obligations to farmers and other landowners, as set out in the long-established Country Code.

Public Transport

The walks in this book are based on the use of a motor vehicle, with a recommendation for car parking in each case. However, there is no doubt that, particularly in an area such as the Lake District, use of public transport is more environmentally friendly and should be encouraged. With that in mind, the following notes are offered to those who prefer to avoid the use of individual vehicles. Full timetables are issued twice each year and may be obtained from Tourist Information Centres or the Cumbria County Council Public Transport Team, Citadel Chambers, Carlisle, tel. 01228 606000.

Rail

For obvious reasons, railway services are generally confined to the edges of the district. The branch line from the West Coast Main Line at Oxenholme to Windermere serves walk no. 7 and, with some extra distance, to walk no. 8. The coastal line from Barrow in Furness to Whitehaven is pleasantly scenic and gives access to walk 14.

Boats

The timetabled services on Windermere link with walk 8 and, with extra distance, walks 5,6, and 7. Similarly, on Derwentwater there is a link with walks 20 and 21; on Ullswater with walks 29 and 30.

Buses

Long distance coaches reach many of the Lake District centres daily from most cities and major towns throughout Britain. Since deregulation several companies provide a wide range of local services, some during summer only and some with very limited frequency. Always consult an up-to-date timetable.

◆ Tyson of Cumbria service 605 – Caldbeck to Wigton, one bus each way on Tuesday only – serves Caldbeck and Hesket Newmarket, walks 27 and 28.

◆ Cumberland 06 – Whitehaven to Ravenglass, no Sunday service – serves Ravenglass, walk 14.

◆ Mackenzie Travel 25 – Workington to Seascale, one bus each way, Monday to Friday – serves Gosforth, walk 15.

◆ Cumberland 555/556 – Lancaster to Carlisle, major service along A591, through the heart of the district – serves Windermere, Ambleside, Rydal, Grasmere, Keswick and, summer only, Bassenthwaite, walks 3, 4, 5, 6, 7, 8, 18, 20, 21, 25.

◆ Cumberland X5 – Whitehaven to Penrith, serves Bassenthwaite and Keswick, walks 18, 20, 21.

◆ Cumberland 79, – Keswick to Seatoller, the Borrowdale bus – serving villages along the valley, walks 20, 21, 22, 23, 24.

◆ Cumberland 77/77A – Keswick to Buttermere, summer only, two buses daily – also serving Seatoller and other villages along Borrowdale, walks 16, 20, 21, 22, 23, 24,

◆ National Trust Landscape 95 – Keswick to Watendlath, summer only – serving walks 20, 21, 24.

◆ Cumberland 76 – Keswick to Bassenthwaite, one bus daily, Monday to Saturday – serving walk 18, 20, 21

◆ Braithwaite's Coaches 100 – Keswick to Thornthwaite, Thursday and Friday only – also serves Braithwaite and Portinscale, walks 19, 20, 21.

◆ Cumberland 73/73A – Keswick to Caldbeck, summer Sundays only, serves walks 20, 21, 26, 27, 28.

◆ Cumberland 505/506 – Bowness to Hawkshead/Coniston to Bowness, frequency varies greatly from summer to winter – also serves Ambleside, walks 5, 6, 8, 10, 11, 13.

◆ Cumberland 516 – Ambleside to Dungeon Ghyll, the Langdale bus – serves walks nos. 5, 6, 12.

◆ Cumberland 599 – Grasmere to Windermere and Bowness Pier, in summer the very frequent open topped bus, much more restricted in winter and from Ambleside to Bowness only – serves walks 3, 4, 5, 6, 7, 8.

◆ Caldew Coaches 620 – Carlisle to Caldbeck, one bus each way on Wednesday only – serves walks 27, 28.

◆ Cumberland 961 – Penrith to Skelton, one bus each way on Tuesday only, also serving Caldbeck and Hesket Newmarket – walks 27, 28

◆Cumberland 108/Postbus 161 – Penrith to Patterdale, also serving Pooley Bridge and Glenridding – walks 29, 30.

◆Cumberland 37 – Workington to Keswick and Patterdale, summer only – serves walks 20, 21, 30.

◆Postbus 110 – Penrith to Martindale, limited service, not on Sunday – serves walk 29.

◆Cumberland 517 – Windermere to Glenridding, summer only – serves walks 7, 8, 30.

◆Cumberland 530/531 – Windermere, Grange and Kendal – serves walks 7, 8, 9.

◆Cumberland 518 – Ambleside and Windermere to Ulverston, not Sunday – serves walks 5, 6, 7, 8,

◆Cumberland 515 – Ambleside to Newby Bridge, also serves Hawkshead and Grizedale, summer only – walks 5, 6, 10, 11.

◆Cumberland 534 – Finsthwaite to Cartmel, summer only – serves walk 9.

◆Muncaster Microbus 14 – Muncaster to Millom, very limited service, weekdays only – serves walk 14.

◆Muncaster Microbus 14 – Muncaster to Gosforth, very limited service, weekdays only – serves walks 14, 15.

◆Cumberland 11/11A – Keswick to Whitehaven and Ravenglass, summer only, Saturday and Sunday – serves walks 14, 15, 20, 21.

◆Muncaster Microbus 13 – Muncaster to Whitehaven, Tuesday and Thursday only – serves walks 14,15.

◆Coast to Coast 491 – Kirkby Stephen to St Bees, one bus each way summer only, passing through Lake District in a large loop, designed especially for walkers – serves walks 3, 4, 5, 6, 16, 20, 21, 29, 30.

◆Cumberland 519 – Kendal to Kentmere, Saturday and Sunday, summer only – serves walk 2.

◆Cumberland 550 – Milnthorpe to Kendal, one bus each way on Wednesday only – serves walk 1.

◆Cumberland 550 – Kendal to Natland, one bus each way on Wednesday only, three buses each way on Saturday, summer only – serves walk 1.

1. Natland and Sedgewick

Length:	5¼ miles.
Summary:	A level walk in an attractive part of the valley of the River Kent, including the villages of Natland and Sedgewick, and close to Sizergh Castle. The towpath of the former Lancaster Canal provides much of the outward route, with the return by a riverside path; there is about 1½ miles on very minor public roads.
Car Parking:	Roadside parking in Natland village, by the church the road is sufficiently wide to avoid causing obstruction. Grid reference 521893.
Map:	Ordnance Survey Outdoor Leisure no. 7, The English Lakes, south-eastern area, 1:25,000 or Landranger no. 97, Kendal to Morecambe, 1:50,000.

Tea Shop

The Barn Tea Room at Low Sizergh Farm is accessed through the artistic craft centre. All the goods are attractively displayed and might

Sizergh Barn tea shop

prove irresistible – especially just prior to Christmas. Low Sizergh is a working farm and the milking parlour is viewed from the tea room. Indeed from about 3.45pm each day one can observe the herd of approximately one hundred and forty Fresian Holstein cows being milked – all highly mechanised and with a modern computer system in operation. The decor of the café is interesting with farming memorabilia; even the crockery has farming motifs.

Food and drink offered is of a high standard. Coffee is served in cafétières, choice of tea including the popular Lakeland blend (said to be especially suited to the local water). Home-made soup is served. Other savoury dishes are available if calling at lunchtime. Tea time temptations include Cumberland Rum Nicky, Borrowdale bread, Westmorland dream cake, or Cumberland currant pasty.

Open: Easter to 31st December 10am to 5pm every day and, from 1st January to Easter, 10.45am to 4.30pm every day but closed on Mondays. Tel: 015395 60426

About the Area

Natland and Sedgewick are pleasing, stone-built, villages with tidy, well-kept, centres. They have both become popular out of town residential areas for nearby Kendal and there has been considerable post-war residential development. The parish church of St Mark, in Natland, is early 20th Century but built in a traditional style.

The southern portion of the Lancaster Canal, built to connect coal fields in the Wigan area with Preston, opened as early in the canal era as 1797, but the northern portion from Tewitfield to Kendal was not completed until June 1819. On the 18th of that month there were great celebrations in Kendal, 10,000 people gathering on Castle Hill and the usual array of dignitaries sitting down for a lavish banquet. The main canal trade was in coal from Lancashire, balanced by the export of Westmorland lime and slate. The growth of industry in Kendal was much stimulated and for some years modest profits were made by the canal company. As with other canals, the arrival of the first railways, such as the Lancaster and Carlisle, today's West Coast Main Line, in 1846, with the Windermere branch passing through Kendal in 1847, started the inevitable slow decline, although there was still a minimal trade after World War II. The death knell was the construction of the M6 motorway in the 1970s and associated improvements to the A590 trunk road, guillotining the canal in several places, and leaving the northern section isolated. The state of the section used in this walk makes recent suggestions for a multi-million pound programme to restore navigation to Kendal seem to be rather optimistic and, arguably, hardly justified.

The Kent may be regarded as Kendal's own river, bringing water from the south-east of the Lake District and, with its principal tributaries the Sprint and the Mint, from the Howgill Fells and other high ground to the north of Kendal, with a short and sometimes turbulent course to Morecambe Bay. The section to the south of the town, traversed by this walk, is among the most attractive, with surging rapids and riverside woodland.

In the 18th and 19th Centuries the quarrying industry in Lakeland needed large quantities of gunpowder, resulting in the construction of several works in the south of the area with sufficient capacity to export the powder nation-wide. This section of the River Kent was used to power no less than three such mills, Old Sedgewick and Bassingill in the second half of the 18th Century and New Sedgewick in the mid 19th Century. One of the former works was on the site now occupied by a substantial caravan site on the west bank of the river.

Sizergh Castle has been the home of the Strickland family for more than 750 years. Founded on an original 14th century pele tower (a defensive fortification built extensively throughout Cumberland and Westmorland during the centuries of cross border raiding by the Scots), much extended in Tudor times. The gardens are also highly regarded. Now managed by the National Trust, the castle is open to the public during the normal Trust season, from the end of March to the end of October, Sunday to Thursday, afternoons only.

The Walk

Walk away from the church towards the through road and turn left, south. Pass Holmes Garden Centre and a large house, Appletree. Turn right into a surfaced lane with footpath signs, keeping left as the roadway forks and soon reaching Cracalt House along an avenue of fine mature trees.

Turn left before the main house to leave the road and pass through a farm gate. Follow the well-defined path along a narrow meadow, close to the hedge. Join a rough roadway at a crude 'footpath' sign. Larkrigg Farm is below to the right. Leave the roadway in a short distance, turning left at a 'bridleway' sign.

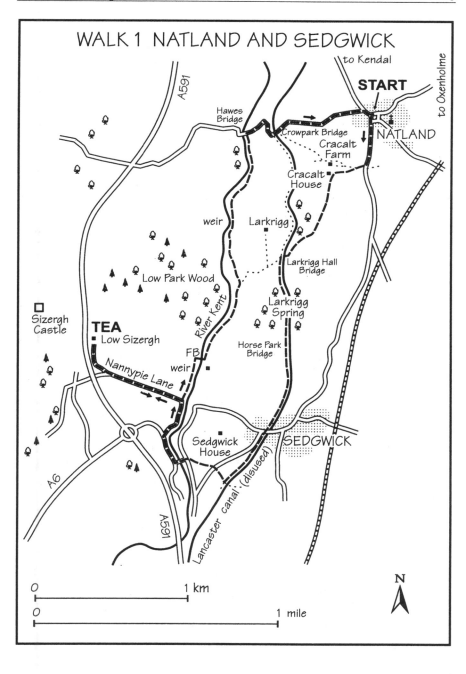

WALK 1 NATLAND AND SEDGWICK

to Kendal

to Oxenholme

A591

START

Hawes
Bridge

Crowpark Bridge

NATLAND

Cracalt
Farm

Cracalt
House

weir

Larkrigg

Larkrigg Hall
Bridge

Low Park Wood

River Kent

Larkrigg
Spring

Sizergh
Castle

TEA

Low Sizergh

FB

weir

Horse Park
Bridge

Nannypie Lane

A6

Sedgwick
House

SEDGWICK

Lancaster canal (disused)

A591

O   1 km

O   1 mile

N

A bridge which spanned the long defunct Lancaster Canal is soon reached, standing forlorn across the part filled canal bed. Cross over and go round to the left to join the former towpath through a squeezer stile. Turn right along the towpath to head for Sedgewick. Apart from a little mud through Larkrigg Spring Wood, this path provides easy walking, excellent underfoot.

Leave the wood at an iron kissing gate and go across a meadow to an even more isolated and incongruous canal bridge. Go under the bridge and continue to Sedgewick. The west coast main railway line is a short distance to the left. The former canal wharf at Sedgewick is now an unfortunate eyesore, but the canal passes high over the otherwise trim stone village. After a sign 'Tewitfields 12, Kendal 3' there is a way down to the village on the right.

Ignore this and continue to the next bridge, with kissing gate. Turn right. Descend through a little meadow and cross a minor road, with kissing gates on each side, shortly joining a more important road at a stile, close to ornamental pillars and railings which are part of the boundary of the grounds of Sedgewick House.

Cross the river on the road bridge and turn right along the road. In 200m, or so, turn right at a road junction. There is a sign 'Farm Shop, Tea Room and Crafts, Low Sizergh Barn'. At the next junction, which has a similar sign, turn left. The barn, including our tea room, is on the right in about half a mile. For Sizergh Castle go under the main A591 road and turn right.

Return along the minor access road to the junction with the tree in the middle and turn left to walk by the side of the river, passing a weir. Turn right to cross the river on a suspension footbridge with a 'public footpath' sign. At the far end of the bridge turn left.

The path, reasonably well-defined, stays quite close to the river. Across the water is the caravan site on land formerly occupied by the gunpowder mill. After a waymarked gate the path broadens into a lane. In a short distance turn left at a squeezer stile in a short section of wall to stay by the river, passing through woodland rich in beech, silver birch and holly.

Natland church is visible to the right before a minor road is joined at a stile, close to a bridge over the river, here flowing deep and fast between constricting rocky sides. Turn right to walk for about half a mile to the village, passing over the former canal bed, greatly infilled. The higher part of Kendal town can be seen away to the left as Natland is reached.

2. Kentmere and Harter Fell

Length: 9 miles.

Summary: A genuine fell walk along the upper part of the Kentmere Valley, to the Nan Bield Pass and then up to the top of Harter Fell, 778m. (2553ft), (Wainwright gives a height of 2539ft), continuing along the broad ridge over Kentmere Pike, 730m (2396ft) as part of the return route. Generally good underfoot for a fell walk, with no significant rock scrambling.

Car Parking: The traditional car parking area in Kentmere is behind the village Institute, close to the church, grid reference 456042. However, this informal area now has a capacity of only 9 or 10 vehicles and is very often inadequate. In recent seasons a nearby field has been used as an overflow, at a moderate charge. There are no public conveniences nearer than Staveley.

Map: Ordnance Survey Outdoor Leisure no. 7, The English Lakes, south-eastern area, 1:25,000 or Landranger no. 90, Penrith and Keswick, 1:50,000.

Tea Shop

Maggs Howe is a real find – way up the Kentmere Valley in a tranquil setting, it is like turning the clock back forty years or so – a rambler's regular refreshment stop where everyone chats about where they have walked that day, be it one mile or twenty.

Very reasonably priced menu with good food and lashings of tea and coffee – just what is needed after a walk on the fells. Roast lunches are served on Sundays but for these, and for evening meals for non-residents, it is necessary to make advance reservations. Bed and breakfast is also available at Maggs Howe.

Open: Times variable – usually open at all times when Mrs Hevey is at home! Tel: 01539 821689

About the Area

There was a time when Kentmere was a quiet, relatively unfrequented valley, well off centre. To some walkers including, it must

Kentmere church and Kentmere Hall farm

be said, the author, it was scarcely part of Lakeland and conse-
quently hardly worth bothering with. How times have changed!

Flanked by high ridges culminating in the amphitheatre around
the reservoir, and with broad green farmland in the lower reaches,
Kentmere now takes its proper place as a valley of considerable
charm, with much to offer for walkers.

Although Harter Fell is a well-rounded mountain when seen from
Kentmere, on the north side, at the head of Mardale, there are great
walls of broken crags. The summit is a gentle grassy plateau,
crowned by a large cairn curiously interlaced with former fence
posts. Kentmere Pike is less impressive; a rather insignificant emi-
nence on the long high ridge which separates Kentmere from Long
Sleddale. However, the Long Sleddale side of the Pike and of its
ridge generally is impressively rocky with high crags and deep gul-
lies.

Human occupation in Kentmere is much as one would expect in a
farming valley, with a small village and the outlying hamlets of
Green Quarter and Hallow Bank. St Cuthbert's Church is mainly of
the 16th century. It is claimed that those carrying the body of the
saint rested in Kentmere overnight on the journey to Durham. Kentmere Hall (farm) near the village is founded on the partial ruin of a
14th century pele tower, constructed, like the others in Cumbria, as
defence against marauding Scots.

At the only entrance by road to Kentmere, Staveley is a large village with plenty of shops and other facilities (including public conveniences!). Formerly an industrial settlement with mills using the
water power of the River Kent and its tributary River Gowan to make
bobbins and for various textile processes, Staveley has become a desirable residential village, particularly since the construction of the
road by-pass a few years ago. There is a station on the Oxenholme to
Windermere branch railway line.

The Walk

Start behind the village institute. Go through a gate signposted 'public footpath to Upper Kentmere, Kentmere reservoir' and follow a
broad gravelled path. Turn right through a small gate before the entrance to a house, then turn left along a surfaced lane, uphill.

Pass across the front of a farm. Green Quarter is the hamlet across
the valley. The lane soon loses its surface. Go through two gates, join

another track and bear left past a farm, with more gates. A footbridge is soon in view to the right. Go through a squeezer stile in the wall and cross the footbridge over the infant River Kent. Go left up the bank and over a stile in the wall at the top. Turn left to follow Low Lane up the valley.

As the lane ends, cross a stream on a bridge and take 'public bridleway, Mardale', forking left. Cross another footbridge and pass below the hamlet of Hallow Bank, bending left to stay close to a wall. Go through a farm gate and pass Overend, an isolated farm.

Just after the farm, turn right, uphill, to leave the cart track at a sign 'Bridleway, Nan Bield Pass, 2¼ miles'. The path is distinct, initially over grass, bearing left to stay quite close to the cart road for some distance. Keep close to a wall on the left, cross a stream and continue to another gate. Cross more streams and continue by the wall.

After crossing a stream with a tiny waterfall the climb starts in earnest with the path winding quite steeply but without real problems underfoot. To the left, Ill Bell is dominant on the long ridge comprising Yoke, Ill Bell and Froswick. Behind, the Kent Estuary portion of Morecambe Bay can be seen.

From the top of the rise carry on across a more level section; the knobble to the right of the path is Smallthwaite Knott. Below is Kentmere reservoir, with the dam now restored after some years of being virtually without water. After passing the Knott there is a slightly downhill length before the final steep zig-zagging rise to the top of the Nan Bield Pass, with its well-constructed stone shelter. From the top there are views over Mardale, including part of Haweswater.

Turn right, uphill, towards Harter Fell. The path weaves its way through the rocky terrain, but without scrambling. Small Water is close below at the foot of precipitous slopes. Behind, Thornthwaite Beacon is the structure visible more than one mile away.

Harter Fell summit is not very exiting; turn right to follow the broad ridge for most of the return. The fence, superseded by a wall in places, is the sure guide to the route along the ridge, a great comfort in mist or after dark. From Harter Fell, the views are extensive; Long Sleddale Fells, the Howgills and the Pennine Hills to the east, Morecambe Bay and Windermere to the south, and Lakeland peaks such as the Coniston group, Bowfell and Scafell to the south west and west.

Walk along the ridge, reaching Kentmere Pike in 1¼ miles, after a

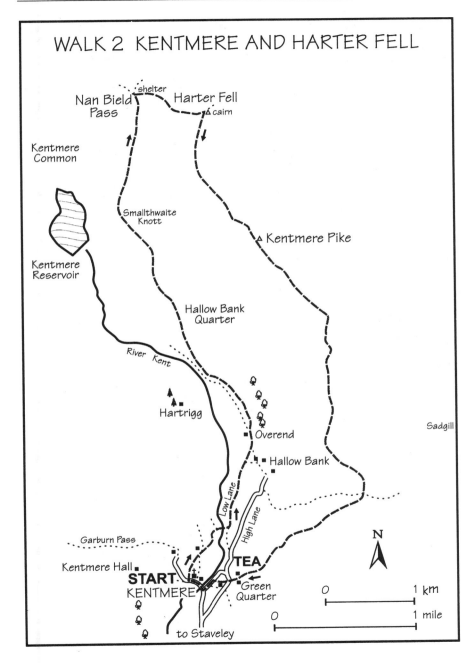

WALK 2 KENTMERE AND HARTER FELL

shelter

Nan Bield
Pass

Harter Fell

△ cairn

Kentmere
Common

Smallthwaite
Knott

△ Kentmere Pike

Kentmere
Reservoir

Hallow Bank
Quarter

River Kent

Hartrigg

Sadgill

Overend

Hallow Bank

Low Lane

High Lane

Garburn Pass

N

Kentmere Hall

TEA

START
KENTMERE

Green
Quarter

0   1 km

0   1 mile

to Staveley

shallow depression. The summit cairn is on a low rocky shelf; there is a triangulation point behind the adjacent wall. Continue along the obvious path, diverging from the fence after half a mile to go over a ladder stile at a cross wall. After the stile the path soon converges with the wall on the left. Rise a little before continuing downhill; the small tarn some distance ahead is Skeggles Water. Descend a rough stony section, close to the wall, keep left at a boggy area, descend a steep, awkward, section, then pass another bog before joining the walkers' highway from Sadgill in Long Sleddale to Kentmere.

This major path is reached close to a farm gate and a junction of walls. Turn left, go through the gate and then turn sharp right to go over a ladder stile. Follow a fairly distinct path to a gate/ladder stile over a cross wall and continue; parts of this track can be muddy in wet weather. There are occasional waymarks on posts before the path begins its descent to Green Quarter and Kentmere.

Turn sharp right at the top edge of Green Quarter, go through a waymarked gate and turn left to take the descending roadway, which soon becomes surfaced. The entrance drive to Maggs Howe is on the left.

From Maggs Howe continue down to a road junction and follow the signpost 'Beckstones, Hallow Bank and Overend'. In 30m go over a signposted stile and descend to woodland, reached at a stile by a rushing little stream. At the minor road at the bottom edge of the wood turn left. At the junction with the valley road turn right to cross the river and return to the parking area.

3. Grasmere and Alcock Tarn

Length:	3¼ miles.
Summary:	A short but quite demanding walk which combines the steep climb to Alcock Tarn, perched high up the valley side, with a gentle stroll through the ever popular Grasmere village. Paths are easy to follow, but are rough, steep and stony in places.
Car Parking:	There are several car parks in Grasmere village and a long layby on the main A591 road just north of the Swan Inn (2 hours limit). The pay and display car park by the Village Hall is recommended. Grid reference 338078.
Map:	Ordnance Survey Outdoor Leisure no. 7, The English Lakes, south-eastern area, 1:25,000 or Landranger no. 90, Penrith and Keswick, 1:50,000.

Tea Shop

Langman's Coffee Lounge, together with the delicatessen, is part of the Harwood Hotel owned and personally managed by Bob and Jackie Langman. Hospitality is historic here for it was one of the first tea rooms in Grasmere. At some time in the past it was a coffee house and reading room, later a temperance guest house; it continues to offer a welcoming atmosphere for refreshment. The furnishings and ambience are good; food and drink is of fine quality.

Coffee – a choice of many blends, teas – all leaf, with a strainer provided, to give the best flavour, fruit teas, herb teas, elderflower or ginger cordial, and Lake District mineral water are all available. Food on the menu is available all day and includes soup, quiche, Cumberland meat platter, filled rolls and sandwiches. Teatime temptations are fresh cream cakes, warm muffins, buttered Borrowdale bread, carrot cake, scones with jam and cream.

Open: 10am to 5.30pm (5pm in winter) every day all the year except Christmas period. Tel: 015394 35248

About the Area

Alcock Tarn, sitting in a shallow depression high on the flank of Heron Pike, is not a particularly pretty sheet of water, but the situation, at a height of 320m (1050ft) is impressive. From close by the tarn the views are wide ranging.

The Heaton Cooper Studio, Grasmere

Grasmere is one of Lakeland's best large villages, close to the heart of the district, but readily accessible from both north and south. The setting, close to its beautiful lake in a most picturesque broad valley ringed by mountains, is superb. In addition to the pleasure of wandering around and possibly enjoying the range of shops in the village, the following might be of interest to visitors:

Parish church of St Oswald. Commenced in 13th century and much modified since. Don't be put off by the drab exterior, inside the church the curiously lopsided effect does not detract from the overall attraction. In the graveyard, soothed by the lapping waters of the River Rothay, lie several of the Wordsworth family, including William himself. Across the road is the Rectory, Wordsworth's home for two unhappy years. The house was damp and two of his children died here at the ages of 3 and 6 years respectively.

Grasmere Gingerbread Shop. Started by Sarah Nelson more than 100 years ago, the gingerbread is still made to a secret recipe. The building was formerly the school house.

Tourist Information Centre, at the far end of the Grasmere Garden Centre.

Heaton Cooper Gallery, facing the Green. Display of the work of several members of the talented Heaton Cooper family with a large variety of prints available.

Dove Cottage and adjacent gallery. Home of William Wordsworth and Dorothy for nine years from 1799 to 1808. Here the young poet came to full maturity during the most productive period of his life. Open to the public all the year round, with the exception of a month in mid-winter.

Boat Landings. Rowing boats for hire just a little way along the road past the garden centre, towards Red Bank and Elterwater.

Additionally, the village hall is the venue for the prestigious Lakeland Artists' summer exhibition and the large field between village and main road is the site of the world famous Grasmere Sports, held in August each year.

The Walk

From the car park by the village hall turn right to head along the road to the Swan Inn, sitting prettily on the far side of the main road, below the slopes and crags of Stone Arthur.

Cross the road and go up the lane to the right of the Inn. Keep left at a fork and then turn right at a sign 'public footpath Greenhead Gill. Alcock Tarn' The surfaced track is now rising, with a rushing stream on the right. Go through a gate at the top of the roadway and turn right immediately to cross Greenhead Gill on a footbridge. This valley is the location for Wordsworth's poem 'Michael'.

A well-used path now climbs away from the gill, by the side of a wall. Below, the line of the Manchester Corporation pipeline from Thirlmere is evident as it bridges the valley bottom. The path winds as it climbs steeply below Butter Crag, always clear on the ground and with the occasional variation, as loops are short cut.

Pass a small pond/boggy area, go over a stile in a wall and reach Alcock Tarn. This is a fine picnic place in good weather and the tarn is said to be popular for bathing. This I have yet to see!

There are two routes down from the tarn. The first goes straight ahead to a stile and continues downhill, steep and stony in places but always easy to follow.

A more attractive route goes through a gap in the wall up to the right from the tarn. This is also the viewpoint from which Windermere, Morecambe Bay, Coniston Old Man, Wetherlam, Crinkle Crags, Bowfell, Langdale Pikes, Helm Crag and Steel Fell can be seen, with the Vale of Grasmere spread out below. From the gap a

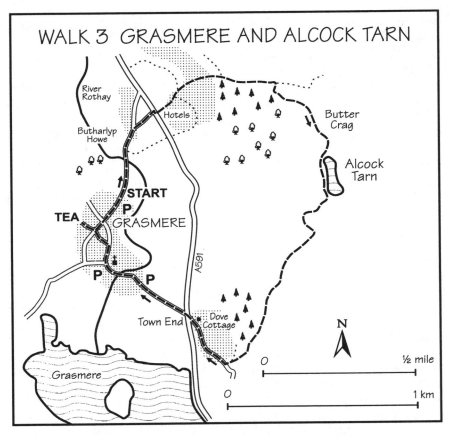

WALK 3 GRASMERE AND ALCOCK TARN

River Rothay

Hotels

Butharlyp Howe

Butter Crag

Alcock Tarn

TEA

START
P
GRASMERE

P

P

A591

Town End

Dove Cottage

Grasmere

N

0   ½ mile

0   1 km

path loops round Grey Crag and crosses the Alcock Tarn outfall stream before passing through tree plantations in its steady descent. From either route the views of the Vale of Grasmere are splendid.

The two paths rejoin a little way before a surfaced roadway is reached, with a well-sited seat above a small pond. Turn right to descend to a minor road junction, keeping right, and downhill, to pass Dove Cottage before reaching the main road. Cross over and follow Stock Lane into Grasmere village. Pass the church and the garden centre and keep left along the main street to the teashop, on the left just before the Red Lion Inn.

Leave the teashop and continue in the same direction, passing the Green and the Heaton Cooper Gallery, to return to the car park.

4. Rydal and White Moss Common

Length: 3 miles

Summary: Including two of Lakeland's best loved footpaths, apart from hill climbing this walk has all the ingredients which make the district so special. Lake, woodland, river and mountain views combine to produce a circuit of spectacular beauty, with the added interest of the Rydal caves. Underfoot, the paths are first class throughout.

Car Parking: National Trust pay and display car park at White Moss Common, between Rydal and Grasmere. On both sides of the main A591 Ambleside to Keswick road. Grid reference (lower side) 350065.

Map: Ordnance Survey Outdoor Leisure no. 7, The English Lakes, south-eastern area, 1:25,000 or Landranger no. 90, Penrith and Keswick, 1:50,000.

Tea Shop

The tea room at Rydal Hall is the only refreshment facility in the village. The Hall is owned by the Carlisle Diocese as a retreat and conference centre. Members of the resident Community staff the little café/kiosk which is unapologetically basic but beautifully set by the side of the tumbling beck, with a lovely terrace. Available are tea, coffee, cold drinks, ice cream, sandwiches and cakes.

Open from Easter to the end of October, 11.00am to 5pm (11.30 to 5pm on Sundays). No telephone no. available.

About the Area

Apart from its undisputed beauty, the Rydal (Rye Dale – the valley where rye is grown) area has much of interest for the visitor.

Rydal Hall was for more than 300 years the seat of the Le Fleming family. In modern times it was purchased by the Diocese of Carlisle and is now used as a conference centre and retreat, with camping site and youth centre in the grounds. The present structure is largely of the 17th century, with a late 18th century facade. An earlier Rydal Hall was sited almost half a mile away on the far side of the main road.

Rydal Mount was the home of William Wordsworth from 1813 until

Rydal Hall

his death in 1850. The house is an 18th century enlargement of a much earlier farmhouse and is open to the public all the year round, apart from a mid winter break of three weeks. The furnishing is much as it was in Wordsworth's time, including family portraits and chair seats embroidered by Mary and Dorothy Wordsworth and Sara Hutchinson. The large garden is attractive, with terraces created by Wordsworth himself and some splendid long views.

Rydal church was originally a chapel, built on her orchard by Lady le Fleming in 1832 at a cost of £1,500. It was enlarged in 1884. Externally the building is unremarkable, but inside the pews occupied by Wordsworth, who was a chapel warden, and Dr. Arnold (of Rugby School fame) can both be identified. The balcony, with its separate entrance, was reserved for the le Fleming family. Various plaques and windows commemorate members of these families.

Behind the church is **Dora's field**, with great banks of daffodils. Wordsworth purchased the field in 1826 when eviction from Rydal Mount by his landlady, Diana le Fleming, seemed likely. He did some work on the design of a house for the site, but when eviction was no longer a threat, he gave the field to his daughter Dora. The celebrated poem has nothing whatsoever to do with these daffodils!

The Walk

Cross the road if parked in the old quarry part of the car park and, from either part, pass the public conveniences and take the broad track close to the side of the River Rothay. Cross the footbridge over the river. The way is straight ahead through Rydal Wood as indicated on the signpost. If desired a diversion to the left can be made to see the wetland conservation area.

The very well used track rises easily among the trees to reach a gate in the top wall. Go through and turn left. There are two good paths to Rydal, that descending by the side of the wall being slightly the shorter. The upper path is recommended for superior views and for a visit to the Rydal caves. This path rises a little at first as it crosses part of the flank of Loughrigg, then maintaining its height above Rydal Water. The views are marvellous; across the lake is the Fairfield group of mountains, ending abruptly with Nab Scar, towering above Rydal. Helm Crag is visible towards Grasmere and the lake itself has a most beautiful setting.

Go over a rocky nobble to reach a former quarrying area, which includes the massive Rydal cave, ahead. From the cave go steeply downhill, passing the lower cave, accessible only to those prepared to climb an awkward little rock face.

At a gate by the near end of woodland, zig zag left and right to descend to the lakeshore. Go through an old iron kissing gate into the Rydal Woods Access Area. Leave the wood by a similar gate and follow the path to a footbridge over the River Rothay. Rise to the main road and turn right for about 120m. Turn left up the cul de sac road leading to Rydal Mount.

On the left is Rydal church, with Dora's field behind. A little further is Rydal Hall; turn right at the second entrance to walk to the tea shop in less than 150m. This track is the only right of way through the grounds of the Hall, but entrance to view the formal gardens, laid out by Thomas Mawson early in the present century, is usually permitted.

Return to the road and turn right, rising to pass Rydal Mount. Turn left at a 'public bridleway, Grasmere' sign to take the old 'corpse' or 'coffin' road. Go through a gate and continue along the excellent track, which rises and falls across the lower slopes of Nab Scar. Wansfell Pike is dominant in the view behind. Apart from the odd stony section, the track is entirely easy.

Thirty metres after a gate turn left down a steep path between widely spaced walls. There is abundant bramble and the accompaniment of a rushing little stream beside the track. Near the bottom the stream joins a bigger stream, with a waterfall. At the main road turn left to return to the lower car park, or right to return to the old quarry car park.

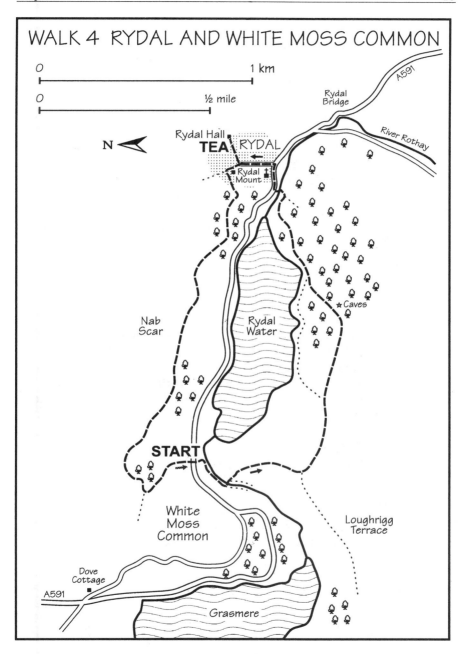

WALK 4 RYDAL AND WHITE MOSS COMMON

0 _____ 1 km

0 _____ ½ mile

A591

Rydal Bridge

River Rothay

N

Rydal Hall

TEA RYDAL

Rydal Mount

Caves

Nab Scar

Rydal Water

START

White Moss Common

Loughrigg Terrace

Dove Cottage

A591

Grasmere

5. Ambleside and Sweden Bridge

Length: 3 miles

Summary   Combining woodland and open fell side in the lower part of the
                  Scandale valley, this is one of the most attractive short low level walks
                  in the district, with High Sweden Bridge as the destination. Although in
                  mountain terms this is a low level walk, there is quite a long steep
                  climb at the outset.

Car Parking   Main pay and display car park, with public conveniences, in Rydal
                  Road, Ambleside. Grid reference 375047.

Map   Ordnance Survey Outdoor Leisure no. 7, The English Lakes, south-
                  eastern area, 1:25,000 or Landranger no. 90, Penrith and Keswick,
                  1:50,000.

Tea Shop

"Coffee Time" is one of many tea shops in Ambleside and can be
found at the top of the town just opposite the shopping precinct.
Very pleasing decor – paintings of local scenes, tea and coffee con-
tainers on shelves round the walls, and a "boot friendly" tiled floor.

A very good choice of tea and coffee is offered. Also there is iced
tea, de-caff coffee, hot chocolate, and cold drinks. To eat there are
toasted sandwiches, savoury specialities, scones, caramel shortbread, and lots of other delectables – the carrot and cream cheese
cake is particularly delicious.

Open: 10am to 5pm all the year – every day in main season but
closed on Fridays during the other months. Tel: 015394 31027

About the Area

The valley of the Scandale Beck lies between the Low Pike/High Pike
ridge which forms one arm of the Fairfield Horseshoe, and the more
gentle side of Red Screes. The eastern side of the latter mountain
towers menacingly over the Kirkstone Pass. The valley carries a
good walkers' route from Ambleside, over the Scandale Pass and
then down Caiston Glen to Patterdale. The first part of this track is
used in the present walk. Arguably, this lower part of the valley,
with its more diverse landscape including small waterfalls, rushing

rapids and two fine old bridges, is considerably more attractive than the rather desolate upper part.

The town of Ambleside is very briefly described in walk no. 6. For more information about the features of the town and a suggested town walk, refer to the author's 'Town and Village Discovery Trails of Cumbria and the Lake District' (Sigma Press).

High Sweden Bridge

The Walk

Leave the car park, cross Rydal Road, and start up the road towards 'Kirkstone', climbing steeply. Pass the Golden Rule Inn, then turn left into Sweden Bridge Lane. Across the valley is the great hump of Loughrigg Fell, well wooded on its lower slopes.

The surfaced lane carries on steeply uphill, straight on at a first junction, then left at a fork. At the top go through a gate. The roadway now loses its surface, continuing as a stony lane between well-spaced stone walls, still rising. Heron Pike at one end of the Fairfield

Horseshoe is seen above Rydal Water. Below is a neat Council housing estate, whilst Ambleside town and Windermere are seen behind.

Eventually the track levels out and then descends a little into the Scandale valley. Skirt along the upper edge of woodland, with the beck below, roaring over rapids after heavy rain. Two long disused quarries are passed on the right. The track is always entirely obvious and no route finding is necessary.

As High Sweden Bridge is approached fork left from the main track. This is a good place for a quiet rest and even to dangle one's toes in the water on a suitable day. Cross the bridge, go through the gate, turn left then right to rise along a path, initially gouged in the hillside. Head for an isolated boulder perched on a bank. In front is the start of the long ridge heading for Fairfield via Low and High Pikes. Continue up the valley side to a ladder stile. The path forks immediately; either will do, but that to the right is probably more official.

Join the main Fairfield Horseshoe path and turn left. This well defined path heads unerringly back towards Ambleside, downhill nearly all the way, with several ladder stiles beside gaps in walls en route. Just over a brow a great panoramic view over Ambleside and the lake opens up. Lower down, on the right, is a 'Manchester Corporation' gate, one of hundreds which mark the line of the great aqueduct which takes water from Thirlmere to satisfy Manchester's thirst.

At the bottom of the descent is Low Sweden Bridge, at the heart of a fine wooded gorge, with noisy tumbling beck. Cross over and go through gates to pass Nook End Farm. Continue along the surfaced roadway, Nook Lane, to pass above Charlotte Mason College, now part of St Martin's College of Lancaster.

Join the Kirkstone Road and turn right to return to the main street. The tea shop is to the left.

WALK 5 AMBLESIDE AND SWEDEN BRIDGE

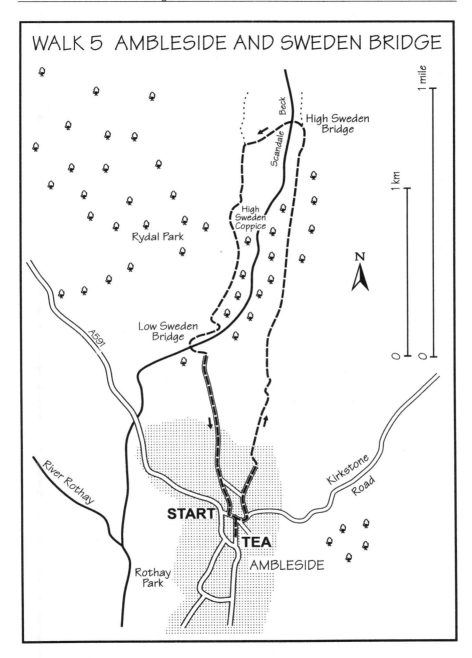

High Sweden
Bridge

Scandale Beck

High
Sweden
Coppice

Rydal Park

Low Sweden
Bridge

A591

River Rothay

START

TEA

Kirkstone
Road

AMBLESIDE

Rothay
Park

N

1 mile

1 km

6. Ambleside and Loughrigg Fell

Length: a) 6½ miles b) 5 miles c) 5 miles at least.

Summary: A choice of walks over one of the district's favourite hills, within easy reach of Ambleside. The ascent totals rather more than 350m (1149ft), some of it quite steep. Good, but occasionally stony and possibly muddy paths. The return includes a length of the very quiet and pleasant Under Loughrigg road.

Car Parking: Any public car park in Ambleside. Directions are given from the main pay and display car park in Rydal Road, with public conveniences, grid reference 375047.

Map: Ordnance Survey Outdoor Leisure no. 7, The English Lakes, south-eastern area, 1:25,000 or Landranger no. 90, Penrith and Keswick, 1:50,000.

Tea Shop

As a major tourist town, Ambleside is almost as well endowed with tea shops and other forms of catering as it is with anorak shops, as a walk along the main street will confirm. For refreshment a little off the beaten track, seek out Rattle Gill, an ancient pedestrian route connecting North Road with the main street. From the line of this walk turn right into North Road, by the Tourist Information Office, then left immediately before the stream.

Rattle Gill Café has been established in an old cottage facing a former mill across the stream. So near to the bustle of the town centre, this is a remarkably peaceful place, welcoming walkers (and their rucksacks) to tea, coffee and cold drinks, with a wide choice of food. A savoury dish of the day is supplemented by soup, filled jacket potatoes, toasted sandwiches and filled baguettes. Cream teas and a good variety of cakes all feature home baking.

On cold days an open fire is a much appreciated feature.

Open: 10.30am to 6pm daily from Easter to end of October and then long weekends during the other months. May be closed for month of January. Tel: 015394 33210

About the Area

Loughrigg Fell is an extensive mass of high ground separating the valley of the River Rothay, with Grasmere and Rydal Water, from the

Bridge over the River Rothay, Ambleside

valley of the River Brathay and Langdale. Despite the modest height of 335m (1101ft) the hill is full of interest, with numerous little rocky tops, cairns and mini tarns, connected by grassy paths winding in all directions through the bracken. Indeed, it could be argued that there are too many paths, leading astray generations of walkers who, having taken Scafell and Great Gable in their stride, feel no need whatsoever for careful route finding on such an insignificant mountain. The three or four main paths are straightforward enough, but many others are discontinuous and misleading. In mist a compass should be carried and used. Like so many intermediate heights, Loughrigg Fell is a fine viewpoint.

Close to the heart of Lakeland, the vibrantly busy little town of Ambleside has always been a favoured visitor centre. Even the Romans built a fort here at Galava, by the lakeshore. The site is in the care of the National Trust and is open to visitors. The Trust's best-known property in Ambleside is Bridge House, oddly constructed astride Stock Ghyll, close to the main car park. The parish church of St Mary is 19th Century, designed by Sir Gilbert Scott. It is generally regarded as rather bland and the provision of a tall spire is certainly questionable in the Lake District. Inside, a large mural of the annual rush-bearing ceremony by Gordon Ransom (1944) and a virgin and child by the celebrated local sculptress Josefina de Vasconcellos are worth seeing.

In 1997 the locally-based Armitt Trust opened its collection of books and Lakeland heritage items, including Beatrix Potter paintings, to the public, in new premises close to the main car park. Old Ambleside, with at least parts of buildings allegedly dating back to the 15th century, is up the hill to the east of the town centre. There is a centrally located Tourist Information Centre.

The Walk

From the Rydal Road car park walk to the main road and turn left. Turn left again shortly to take the footpath beside Stock Ghyll, soon reaching the River Rothay, crossed by a lovely arched footbridge. Turn right along the Under Loughrigg road for about 50m, then turn left over a cattle grid at a 'public bridleway' sign. A surfaced roadway rises steeply with a rushing little stream beside. As height is gained the views are into the heart of the Fairfield Horseshoe of mountains and back over the rooftops of Ambleside, with Wansfell Pike looming above.

Leave the road to the left to climb steps over a wall at a 'Clapper-sgate 1' signpost. Go through a tight squeezer stile, cross a stream and fork right in a few metres to continue uphill on a grassy track through the bracken. After passing a tiny pond, Lily Tarn is soon reached. Go up the bank to the left for grand views to the south, particularly over Windermere, and to Wetherlam, near point of the Coniston Fells.

Descend the bank and bear right to pass the tarn. From here to the summit of Loughrigg Fell a well used permissive path heads in a generally north-westerly direction and can be followed without difficulty, The nature of the fell top, with its innumerable humps and hollows is now very evident. The path runs alongside an old wall for some distance, descending to a kissing gate in a fence, with a glimpse of Loughrigg Tarn below.

As the track bends to the right, there is another wall on the left for a short distance. Cross a tiny stream and continue uphill. Go straight across a well-used path, with a pond on the right, to a large cairn. Ahead, one version of the path goes over a scrambly little knobble, but a slight detour to the left is preferable, the path soon becoming broader and well cairned. The two versions rejoin in a few hundred

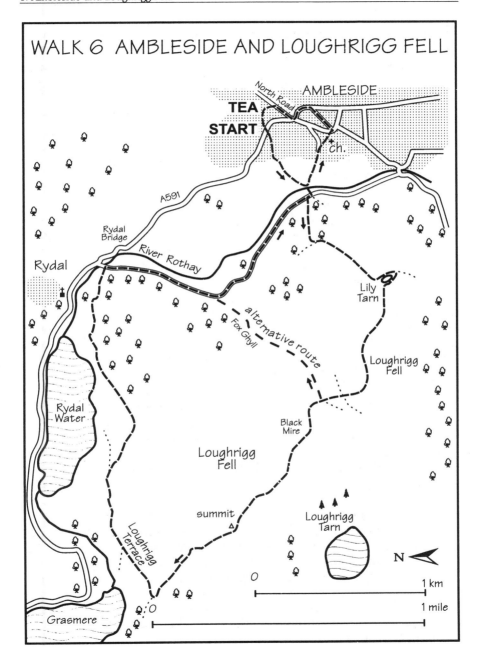

WALK 6 AMBLESIDE AND LOUGHRIGG FELL

AMBLESIDE

North Road

TEA

START

ch.

A591

Rydal
Bridge

River Rothay

Rydal

Lily
Tarn

alternative route

Fox Ghyll

Loughrigg
Fell

Rydal
Water

Black
Mire

Loughrigg
Fell

summit

Loughrigg
Tarn

Loughrigg
Terrace

N

0

0

1 km

1 mile

Grasmere

metres, just below the now obvious summit, with its stone-built Ordnance Survey trig point.

The views are extensive, including many of the great mountains, Windermere, Thirlemere (just!), Grasmere, Wrynose Pass and the Langdale and Rothay valleys.

For the longest return option, carry on in the same direction to descend, steep in places, to Loughrigg Terrace, most famous of all the above-lake footpaths, and turn right to savour this stroll with incomparable picturesque views over William Wordsworth country. At the junctions where paths from the White Moss area join on the left, keep right to take the higher of the two paths above Rydal Water, leading to Rydal Caves, as in walk no. 4.

Descend below the caves; go through the gate just after the seat and continue along the roadway past dwellings to join the Under Loughrigg road by Pelter Bridge. Turn right to follow the delightful road, passing Fox How built, with advice from Wordsworth, by Dr. Arnold, the celebrated headmaster of Rugby school. Cross the bridge over the River Rothay and turn right at once over a flat bridge. Cross Rothay Park, pass the parish church and bear right across the bottom of Compston Road into Church Street. At the top of Church Street turn left. Turn right, into North Street, by the T.I.C. And then left immediately before the stream, into Rattle Gill. On leaving the tea shop, continue back to main street and on to the car park.

For return option b), retrace the outward path for more than three-quarters of a mile. Turn left at a major cross path which soon runs close to a wall on the right before descending steeply alongside a stream in its helter-skelter rush to join the River Rothay. Pass through rhododendron and above the multitude of chimneys of the house named Fox Gill, join the Under Loughrigg road and turn right to return as above.

Return option c) is for the more adventurous who would like to sample some of the many minor paths which criss-cross Loughrigg. From the summit head a little south of east to find a different and meandering route to the Fox Gill path, mentioned in option b), above or, alternatively, head a little north of east to descend to the Rydal area, to join the Loughrigg Terrace to Rydal path near the caves. There are paths available across the intervening area but they are often discontinuous and there is a great deal of boggy ground. In mist a compass is essential. In either case the continuation is as set out in option a), above.

7. Windermere and Orrest Head

Length:	3¼ miles
Summary:	An interesting circuit, largely through Windermere local farming land, also including the village centre and the fine nearby viewpoint of Orrest Head. Good paths and surfaced lanes; mud at Common Farm in wet weather.
Car Parking:	Large pay and display car park off Broad Street, Windermere village centre. Grid reference 413983.
Map:	Ordnance Survey Outdoor Leisure no. 7, The English Lakes, south-eastern area, 1:25,000 or Landranger no. 97, Kendal to Morecambe, 1:50,000.

Tea Shop

David Howarth, his wife Gillian, and all his family are well known in the Windermere area so this café is popular with locals as well as visitors. The menu has many temptations; a warm cheese scone topped with cheese and ham, home made quiche with salad, or more substantial fare such as beef casserole served with a jacket potato and pickled beetroot. For traditional tea try the home made scones, cakes, and a selection of sandwiches. Various blends of tea are available and a choice of filter, expresso, or cappuccino coffees is offered. Very pleasant decor with Renoir prints on the walls – friendly service – reasonable prices.

Open: 10am to 5pm daily all the year – closed Christmas Day and Boxing Day. Tel: 015394 44863

About the Area

Windermere is probably the best known of all Lake District place names, applying both to England's biggest lake and to the large village/small town which grew rapidly adjacent to the station after the arrival of the railway in 1847. For the purpose of this walk it is the village with which we are concerned.

Despite having large numbers of visitors, both staying and daily, unlike Bowness Windermere is not really a holiday resort. There are, however, several catering establishments and a good range of shops, including a modest supermarket and the celebrated Lakeland Ltd. (formerly Lakeland Plastics) by the station. The village centre is essentially a Victorian settlement, with rather drab stone buildings

The countryside close to Windermere is entirely typical of the soft, Silurian period landscape of the south Lakeland fringe, extensively farmed with sheep and some cattle. Orrest Head is surprisingly close to the village. Although only 238m (781ft) in height, it is a lovely viewpoint and was claimed by the late A. Wainwright, legendary walker and author of mountain guide books, to have given him an overwhelming revelation of the area's natural beauty, on his first visit as a young man.

Street scene, Windermere

The Walk

From the car park turn right, along Broad Street, away from the village centre. Turn right at Woodland Road, then left in 40m into Park Road. Turn left through the impressive gate pillars, with plaques recording the efforts of Dr. Hamilton in establishing Queen's Park.

Cross the park, pass the pavilions and walk for a few metres alongside Mill Beck. School Knott rises over the houses, ahead. Cross the bridge and turn right along Droomer Drive, a residential road. Pass a road junction and continue uphill, with the beck still on the right. Take the first turn on the right, a residential cul de sac which continues as a track leaving the built-up area. Cross the beck again by an old stone bridge.

Turn left beyond the bridge, still on a surfaced road. Turn left at a house called Gill Droomer Stile, cross the beck and go over a ladder stile. Turn right, along a narrow footpath to the railway line. Cross with care and follow the just visible path over grass, heading for the end of a wall. The hill on the far side of A591 is Bannerigg.

Go over a ladder stile and take the farmer's wheeled track to the right. As walls converge go through the gate on the right and stay with the farm track to the main road, reached at a gate. Turn right along the generous roadside footpath for less than 100m, quite enough on this busy road, cross over and turn left into the surfaced lane leading to Common Farm. Grove Farm is prominent below Bannerigg, to the right.

Pass The Common, a private residential area, on the way to The Common Farm. At Common Farm turn left at a 'public footpath' signpost, then right, through a waymarked gate. Descend past further farm buildings to a gate on the right at the far end. Bear left, along a walled lane.

In about 300m go over a stile in the wall on the left, then another stile in about 40m to join a footpath by a wall. Continue by the wall, go over another stile and angle left to reach an awkward stile over another wall, soon descending a little to join a cross path.

Turn left. There is a small reservoir here and The Causeway Farm behind. The climb over short grass to the summit of Orrest Head is fairly obvious, never far from the wall on the right. Go over a stile in a cross wall to reach the uncultivated summit area. The top is well provided with seats and has an excellent viewing table. The views are splendid, with the lake, Windermere and Bowness villages and a mountain panorama ranging from Coniston Old Man to Fairfield, with many fine peaks between including Scafell Pike, Great Gable, Bowfell and the Langdale Pikes.

Descend to the right and turn left towards Windermere. Go through an old iron kissing gate with a stone on the far side in memory of Arthur Henry Heywood of Elleray, who dedicated Orrest Head for the use of the public for ever. As the path divides keep straight on down with a wall close on the right. Go left at a 'Windermere village' sign to follow a broad track through an area of rhododendrons. Reach a surfaced road by Elleray Wood Cottage and follow its sinuous windings down to the A591 main road.

Cross to the National Westminster Bank and go down Victoria Street to the village centre. Either of the two main shopping streets will suffice; Renoirs is at the far end, on the right, close to the filling station.

From the tea shop cross the road and proceed along Broad Street, opposite, to the car park.

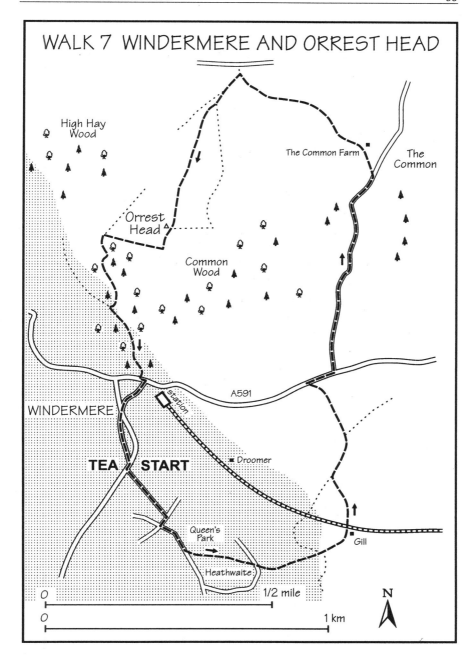

WALK 7 WINDERMERE AND ORREST HEAD

High Hay Wood

The Common Farm

The Common

Orrest Head

Common Wood

WINDERMERE

station

A591

Droomer

TEA · START

Queen's Park

Gill

Heathwaite

O   1/2 mile

O   1 km

N

8. Bowness on Windermere and Brant Fell

Length:	3 miles
Summary:	A short walk, readily combined with enjoyment of the attractions of Bowness. Quiet and attractive countryside, away from the hurly-burly, is very quickly reached. Brant Fell is not a taxing climb and the views from the top make the effort worthwhile. Good and varied footpaths and half a mile of very minor road.
Car Parking:	Use one of the several pay and display car parks in Bowness, the nearer to the centre of the village the better. The large car park on Rayrigg Road is well placed for the tea shop. Grid reference 403972.
Map:	Ordnance Survey Outdoor Leisure no. 7, The English Lakes, south-eastern area. 1:25,000 or Landranger no. 97, Kendal to Morecambe, 1:50,000.

Tea Shop

The Tailor of Gloucester Tea Room at The World of Beatrix Potter, The Old Laundry, in Bowness is a most charming tea room. The lighting is attractive – furniture and crockery of good quality whilst the tiled floor confirms that there are no problems for those wearing walking boots. Lots to look at whilst enjoying welcome refreshment following the walk – needless to say the decor is based very much on Beatrix Potter characters.

There is the usual range of food including "blackboard specials" each day. For tea there are scones, cakes, tea, coffee, cold drinks – lots to choose from here!

The World of Beatrix Potter exhibition is well presented and a worthwhile visit for all age groups but especially magical for children. The Old Laundry Theatre is superb; should there be a production running, try not to miss it!

Open: every day 10am to 5.30pm Easter to end of October. Every day 10am to 4.30pm November to Easter. Tel: 01539 88444

Boats and "cushion huts", Bowness

About the Area

Brant Fell is a modest hill of 191m (627ft) dignified by an entry in the late A. Wainwright's 'Outlying Fells of Lakeland' book. The south side of the top is surprisingly rocky and could give pleasure to those who enjoy rock scrambling. Proximity to Windermere results in fine views over the great majority of the lake, the Coniston and Fairfield fells and, in clear weather, distant Pennine hills beyond Kendal.

The countryside is entirely typical of the relatively soft, 'Silurian', landscape of the southern part of the district, the impact of little rock outcrops being softened by abundant gorse and other vegetation. The area is farmed by the Matson Ground Estate Co.

For most people Bowness hardly needs description. The present jolly, brash, holiday resort is superimposed on an old lakeside fishing and boating community which, with some 17th century buildings, is still evident behind St Martin's church, largely 15th century with a not unattractive 19th century restoration. The church, if open, is well worth a visit. Don't miss the east window, with some glass salvaged from Cartmel Priory following the Dissolution, and the wooden statue of the patron saint.

Between ancient and modern Bowness, the 19th century brought wealthy industrialists, primarily from the Manchester area, after the Windermere branch railway line opened in 1847. Grand houses were constructed, such as the present Belsfield Hotel, for some years the home of the legendary H.W. Schneider, one of the great figures of the iron/steel/ armaments industry at Barrow in Furness.

Modern attractions include the Beatrix Potter Experience, the Steamboat Museum and the water based activities in Bowness Bay.

The Walk

From whichever car park, leave Bowness along the Kendal Road, starting opposite the church. Turn left in a few metres to climb steeply up Brantfell Road. At the top of the road, on the left, is the derelict site of the former Bowness gas works. What a job for the horses which hauled the coal carts up this fearsome hill!

Continue along the footpath, the start (or the finish) of the 72 mile Dales Way long distance path from Ilkley in West Yorkshire to Bowness. Rise quite steeply across a meadow, past a stone seat commemorating the Dales Way. After a kissing gate, turn right along a broad trackway, now rising more gently through woodland, with views over the rooftops of busy, bustling, Bowness, calm and peaceful at this range. Note the substantial stone bench seats provided, presumably by a benevolent land owner, on the left of the track, probably before there were trees on the right.

At the top of the track go through a kissing gate and ascend the little knoll of Post Knott, a much-loved local viewpoint with two seats, the higher having a plaque ' Centenary of National Trust, 1895 – 1995'. The lower seat has lost most of its view during the last few years. From Post Knott bend a little left towards the now obvious summit of Brant Fell, over a ladder stile with a notice 'Access by permission of land owner. Please follow cairns'.

As the grassy track forks, keep left, soon bearing right to climb to the top of the hill by the cairns, as requested, and enjoy the splendid view. Bits and pieces of railing and old foundations mark the site of a former summerhouse, destroyed in a fire many years ago. Brantfell Farm is close below.

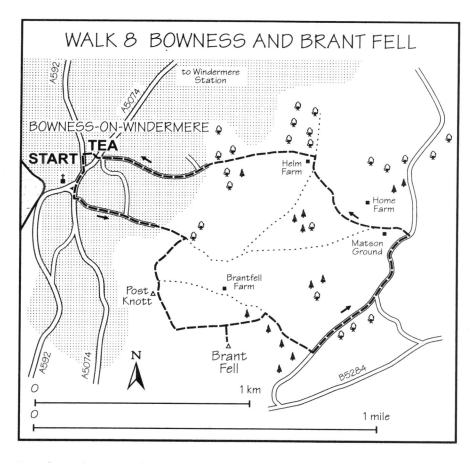

WALK 8 BOWNESS AND BRANT FELL

Head north-east to leave Brant Fell, broadly aiming towards the Matson Ground farm complex, a cluster of white buildings, and follow the cairns to find a lightly used path descending through the conifer plantation. Join a broad farm track and turn right, soon reaching a stile by a gate. Go over and turn left along a very minor road.

Stay with the road for about half a mile to Matson Ground Farm, following 'Heathwaite' at the road junction before the farm. Note the Victorian letter box in the wall by the first farm entrance. Immediately after the second farm entrance, turn left at a 'Dales Way' sign-posted kissing gate and stay beside the fence to another kissing gate. Cross a farm roadway to another kissing gate and a post with two waymarks. Go right here, join the roadway for a few metres and then bear left to a waymarked kissing gate.

The next waymark is on a post 50m ahead. The former Helm Farm, now converted into holiday apartments, is soon in view. Head for it via another waymarked kissing gate. To the right of the buildings go through a kissing gate and then ahead along a vehicular track, soon bending left past a plantation of young trees. Helm Farm carries a date of 1691, a time of much rebuilding and improvement of Lakeland farms, sheep farming then being relatively prosperous.

The roadway soon becomes surfaced, descending along the edge of residential Windermere, (including the authors' home), with fine lake views over the rooftops. At two junctions keep straight on before bending right to descend more steeply down Helm Road to Crag Brow, the main street of Bowness. The tea shop, part of the Beatrix Potter Experience complex, can be accessed either by crossing the road and turning right, uphill, for a short distance, or by descending and turning right into Rayrigg Road, at the mini roundabout.

The suggested car park is very close to the Rayrigg Road entrance to the tea shop.

9. Cartmel and Hampsfield Fell

Length:	5 miles
Summary:	An interesting walk on the fringe of the Lake District based on Cartmel, a gem of a village. The route over Hampsfield Fell (Hampsfell to locals), a limestone ridge 221m (727ft) in height provides fine views over Morecambe Bay and to the Lakeland mountains. The lower part of the walk, returning to Cartmel, has a few potentially muddy areas and several awkward stiles. Roadside walking is minimal and on very quiet lanes.
Car Parking:	Signposted car park, with honesty box, at racecourse on western fringe of Cartmel village. Grid reference 378788.
Map:	Ordnance Survey Outdoor Leisure no. 7, The English Lakes, south-eastern area, 1:25,000 or Landrangers no. 96, Barrow in Furness or 97, Kendal to Morecambe, 1:50,000.

Tea Shop

The chosen venue is The Mallard Tea Shop, opposite the priory church. There is an extensive menu with a choice of the usual light meals including salads, sandwiches, and filled baked potatoes. For tea, scones with jam and cream, crumpets, hot buttered toast, or cakes may be more appealing. Freshly ground coffee, speciality teas, ice cream and milk shakes are available. There is a "Ducklings" menu for children and even the tablecloths have a design including mallards. Service helpful and friendly. Limited number of tables outside.

Open: 10am to 5pm every day all the year except Christmas Day and Boxing Day. Tel: 015395 36800

About the Area

For many years Cartmel was one of the Lake District's well kept secrets. Whilst Grasmere and Hawkshead almost disappeared under tides of visitors, Cartmel remained peaceful, a destination for the discerning few. Cartmel is now much better known and its delightful square and little streets can be busy in season.

The Priory church is a fine building, rescued for parish use at the time of King Henry VIII's dissolution of the monasteries in 1539. The diagonal setting of the belfry of 1410 on the squat central tower is unusual; look also for the holes in an external door, resulting from shots fired at or by Cromwell's troops when they camped in the building for a night in 1643. There was further vandalism inside the church at that time. Go through the Norman doorway to the light and lofty interior and don't miss the 'Holy Family' by the Ambleside sculptress Josefina de Vasconcellos, the Cavendish memorial and a brass plaque in memory of Roland Briggs. The 17th century oak chancel screen and the 15th century miseres on the seats in the choir stalls are a testimony to the craft and the imagination of the medieval woodcarvers. Also surviving the Dissolution is the former **Priory gatehouse**, now in the care of the National Trust, used for exhibitions. It is the most imposing feature of the square, which also has old fish cleaning slabs, the remains of the market cross, inns and interesting shops, including a comprehensive second-hand bookshop.

The **race course** is one of Britain's smallest, allegedly founded by the Priory monks to provide recreation at Whitsun. The Bank Holiday meetings are popular festive occasions, bringing crowds from far and wide.

The **'hospice'** on Hampsfield Fell is a simple square structure provided by a pastor of Cartmel in the mid 19th century. The flat roof has a view indicator. Inside, there are texts on all four walls, including: 'All persons visiting this 'hospice' by permission of the owner, are requested to respect private property, and not by acts of wanton mischief and destruction show that they possess more muscle than brain. I have no hope that this request will be attended to, for as Solomon says "though thou shouldest bray a fool in a mortar among wheat with a pestle, yet will not his foolishness depart from him" G. Remington'. So much for the pastor's view of contemporary humanity! On a clear day, the views extend as far as Skiddaw and Helvellyn in the Lake District, with the Howgill and Pennine Fells to the north-east and east.

The Walk

Walk back to the village square and turn left under the Priory gatehouse. Follow the road round to the right to pass behind the Priory church and reach the main through road. Turn left for 30m and then right, up a few steps, to take the signposted path to 'Hospice and Hamps Fell ¼'.

Cross a large field, keeping fairly close to the right hand boundary. After a 'Hamps Fell' signpost go left then right to pass Pit Farm. Go through a signposted kissing gate and then straight on with a fence on the right. Follow the field boundary to reach another gate. Go through and continue uphill along a well-worn path over grass.

At another signpost carry on, now with a wall on the left. After an-

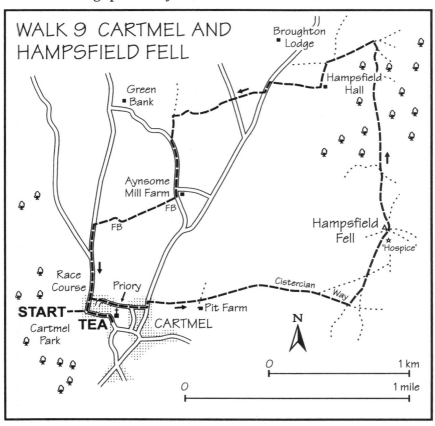

WALK 9 CARTMEL AND
HAMPSFIELD FELL

JJ
Broughton
■ Lodge

Hampsfield
Hall

Green
■ Bank

Aynsome
Mill Farm
FB

FB

Hampsfield
Fell
☆ 'Hospice'

Q Race
Course

Priory

Cistercian

Way

START

Cartmel TEA
Cartmel
Q Park

CARTMEL

■ Pit Farm

N

0   1 km

0   1 mile

other kissing gate the path steepens. Ignore any minor paths to left or right and continue to the top of the broad ridge, where there is a major crossing of paths at a waymarked post. Turn left to head for the now obvious 'hospice', with superb views in either direction.

From the 'hospice' continue along the broad ridge, covered by limestone pavement and mini scarps. The path soon bears a little to the left, along the Cartmel side of the ridge. Note - Early in 1998, footpath diversion notices had been posted; follow any new signposting. The green dotted line right of way shown on Ordnance Survey maps is no longer valid; it ends at a high cross wall with no stile or gate. The correct path crosses the wall at a rather awkward stile and continues attractively along the edge of a conifer plantation. The high ground ahead is Newton Fell.

Pass above Hampsfield Hall farmstead before descending, left, to a gate in the angle of two walls. Go through and keep to the edge of the field, bearing left to stay close to the fence and then head down to an obvious gate in the bottom corner of the field. Go along the farm track and pass through the farm by either of the signposted routes. Turn right along the farm access roadway to reach the public road.

The grand house to the right is Broughton Lodge. Turn left along the road, pass the Broughton Lodge entrance gates and turn right immediately, at a 'public footpath' sign, over an awkward stile, the first of several, to walk along the edge of the field. Cross a minor road, with stiles on each side, and continue along the edge of another meadow to reach a stream with two little bridges. Go through the adjacent squeezer stile, over another stile and cross a narrow meadow to enter woodland.

Bear a little to the right, then left, on vague paths, to a stile at the far edge of the wood. Turn left after the stile to head for a gate. Join a minor public road and turn left, soon passing the Aynsome Manor Hotel. Go straight ahead at a road junction. In a further 100m or so, turn right at a 'public bridleway' sign, crossing a potentially muddy area and keeping the field boundary on the left. The Priory church is in view across the fields.

Go through a farm gate and continue, now with a wall on the right, descending towards a stream and bearing right to cross a footbridge. Rise across the meadow opposite to a gate, giving access to a minor road. Turn left towards Cartmel, passing the racecourse before reaching the village square and visiting the recommended tea shop.

The return to the car park past the village stores is obvious.

10. Hawkshead and Hawkshead Moor

Length:　　　3¾ miles.

Summary:　　A circuit over field and forest paths, visiting Hawkshead village for refreshment. Apart from some likely mud, there are no difficulties, but the return to the car park has a steady ascent of about 130m (430ft). Less than 400m is along a quiet road.

Car Parking:　Official Forest Enterprises car park (free) at Moor Top, well signposted. Accessed by the minor road from Hawkshead to Grisedale, climbing steeply through Roger Ground. Grid reference 344965.

Map:　　　　Ordnance Survey Outdoor Leisure no. 7, The English Lakes, south-eastern area, 1:25,000 or Landranger no. 97, Kendal to Morecambe, 1:50,000.

Tea Shop

Hawkshead is certainly not short of tea shops; we have chosen two, one for each walk and of course the cafés are interchangeable – useful if one is closed on the day you have chosen for your walk.

Grandy Nook, a café with a justifiably good reputation, is tucked away on Vicarage Lane in the centre of this lovely village. John and Lorraine Green run this very friendly tea shop with enthusiasm. Leaf tea served is the Lakeland special blend, which is well suited to the type of water here in the Lake District; of course tea strainers are provided. Light meals such as salads, jacket potatoes, toasted sandwiches, are all listed on the menu. Delicious cakes and scones are served; especially recommended is the warm ginger cake served with local rum butter.

Open: February to November – 10.30am to 5pm but closed on Tuesdays. December and January open Fridays, Saturdays, and Sundays only. Tel: 015394 36404

About the Area

Hawkshead village is described in walk no. 11. Hawkshead Moor is high ground towards the northern end of the huge forested area centred on Grisedale, where there is a comprehensive visitor centre and the enterprising 'Theatre in the Forest'. The whole is managed by

Forest Enterprises, successor to the Forestry Commission. In recent times a shift of emphasis seems to have brought about an encouraging 'walkers welcome' philosophy to the considerable areas of forest managed by Forest Enterprises.

Those (including the author) who are not enthusiastic about long treks through monotonous woodland need have no fear about the walk set out below, little more than one mile of which is in the forest. In any case, since the bad old days of regimented planting of single species conifers, more enlightened policy now produces more diversification and more attractive woodland overall.

Place names 'Roger Ground' and 'Walker Ground' feature in this circuit. In Lakeland, on the dissolution of the monasteries by King Henry VIII's commissioners in 1539/40, comparatively small parcels of the vast estates of Furness Abbey were sold off to individuals. Many, particularly around Hawkshead, were then named after the purchaser, e.g. the ground bought by Roger – Roger's Ground. Surprisingly these original names have survived nearly 450 years to the present day.

Grandy Nook tea room

The Walk

The walk is set out starting from the car park at Moor Top, so that the visit to Hawkshead and the tea shop stop are half way round the circuit. The advantage is that for most of the year Hawkshead is a very busy place, with great pressure on the pay and display car park. To arrive at the village without the encumbrance of a motor vehicle may result in a feeling of superiority over the lesser mortals who are queuing hopefully by the car park entrance and then shuttling only to and from the many clothing shops! The disadvantage is that the uphill part of the walk comes after the refreshment break.

From Moor Top, take the broad forest roadway, passing round the

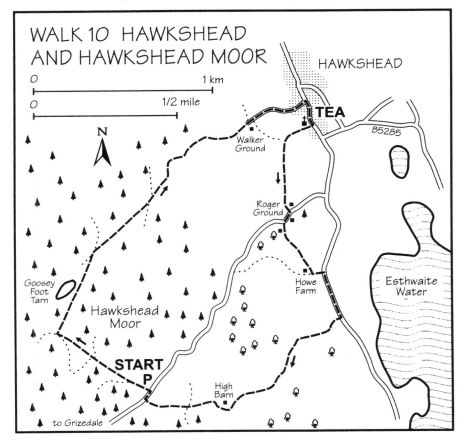

vehicular barrier. At a junction with cycle route signposting go straight ahead to follow the red arrow. This part of the forest is Hawkshead Moor. At the next junction go straight ahead to take an uphill, stony, path, with yellow arrow waymark. Join another forest roadway and then turn right in 30m. Both these junctions are way-marked.

The broad track rises a little further, passing a small tarn, with dam, below on the left. There are soon views ahead, to the mountains behind Ambleside, including Wansfell and the Fairfield Horseshoe and, from a little further on, Ambleside itself. Although the forest is mainly coniferous, there is sufficient variety to avoid monotony. The views extend to include the long ridge of Yoke, Ill Bell and Froswick, leading to High Street. The water in view is the northern end of Windermere.

On reaching a more open area, turn right to leave the forest road-way and take a waymarked stony track, slightly downhill. Join another forest roadway and turn left. In not much more than 100m turn right to continue downhill along the waymarked bridleway along the edge of the woodland, with a stone wall to the right. Esthwaite Water is in view to the right.

Cross a stream, go through a kissing gate, and continue the descent along a delightful track by the side of the stream. Latterbarrow (see walk no. 11) is obvious ahead as Hawkshead is approached. Pass the old house at Walker Ground and follow the white arrow to 'Hawkshead village' along the surfaced access roadway. Reach the village along Vicarage Lane, by Ann Tyson's Cottage. Grandy Nook tea-room is immediately on the right 'walkers welcome, rucksacks and muddy boots included'.

The main car park, public conveniences and the tourist information centre are to the right along the main street.

Start the return by heading past the Old Grammar School up to the church. Fork left in the churchyard to head for a gate in the far boundary, along the side of a fine example of the local slate on edge walling. In 60m go through a kissing gate, turning left to another kissing gate in 40m.

Continue along the bottom edge of a field, through another kissing gate and along a narrow lane to Roger Ground hamlet and a public road. Turn right, uphill, for 100m then left at a road junction. There is a 'Howe Farm' signpost. After passing Springfield cross a stream on a gated footbridge and follow the path past a small static caravan site. Esthwaite Water is in view ahead. At Howe Farm follow the footpath sign to go through two gates and reach the farm access road. Turn left to the public road.

Turn right and walk along the road for less than 400m. Take the second access drive on the right, at a 'public footpath' sign. Pass through a small hamlet with some old buildings and through the grounds of the last house, Elder Ghyll, to commence the steady ascent to Hawkshead Moor. Cross a vigorous beck on a footbridge and continue up the attractively wooded little valley.

Leave the woodland at a gate/stile, cross a tributary stream and follow the waymarks on posts up the open hillside. This path is well waymarked throughout. As height is gained the views become quite extensive, with Esthwaite Water close at hand and the great ring of mountains behind Ambleside and Troutbeck more distant.

Continue through a gate in a wall, soon reaching an isolated dwelling, High Barn. Pass between the house and its outbuilding and then follow its access roadway as it rises steadily to the Hawkshead to Grisedale road. Turn right at the road to return to the car park in 40m.

√ 11. *Hawkshead and Latterbarrow*

Length:	4 miles
Summary:	A circular walk based on Hawkshead, including the popular little summit of Latterbarrow, a noted viewpoint. Much of the walk is through the Claiffe Heights woodland. Paths are generally good and the ascent of Latterbarrow is not too demanding.
Car Parking:	Pay and Display car park in Hawkshead village. Grid reference 353981.
Map:	Ordnance Survey Outdoor Leisure no. 7, The English Lakes, south-eastern area, 1:25,000 or Landranger no. 97, Kendal to Morecambe, 1:50,000.

Tea Shop

The chosen tea shop for this walk is Whigs in the centre of Hawkshead. A whig, similar to a small roll but with caraway seeds which give a very distinctive flavour, is an old (almost extinct!) traditional cake. When Tom and Brenda Seddon started their tea room, Brenda found a recipe for Hawkshead Whigs – hence the name of the café. Reputedly "whig" means spirit or God and these cakes were traditionally baked for Easter like the hot cross bun. They are delicious served toasted and spread with butter. Apart from whigs, there is a good extensive menu here with a choice of coffees, teas, home-made lemonade and lots of other drinks. Wines and beers available only with meals. Numerous savoury dishes are served with whigs including garlic mushrooms or egg and bacon. Main dishes available include Waberthwaite ham with Cumberland sauce, salad, and jacket potato, or local trout with herb potatoes. Good selection of sandwiches, scones, cakes, and Windermere tea bread. Pleasant service – subdued classical background music – some outside tables.

Open: 10.30am to 4.30pm every day except Thursdays all the year. Tel: 015394 36614

About the Area

Hawkshead village is more fully described, with a walking trail, in the author's 'Town and Village Trails of Cumbria and the Lake District' (Sigma Press). Suffice it to say here that despite the pressures of modern tourism, this former market town is still like nowhere else in Lakeland. White painted shops and cottages cluster around linked squares, narrow cobbled streets and alleyways, whilst old inns compete with tea and coffee shops to provide refreshments. The former grammar school had William Wordsworth as its most famous pupil with his initials carved upon a desk as an attraction for visitors. The school is open to the public from Easter to October, Mondays to Saturdays from 1000 to 1700, Sundays 1300 to 1700, with lunchtime closure from 1230 to 1330 on weekdays. His lodgings at Ann Tyson's Cottage can still be seen although the house is not open to the public.

The church is justifiably famous, with a 700 year old tower, a nave extended in about 1300, and side aisles added about 1500. The former white-painted roughcast covering – Wordsworth's 'snow white church upon her hill' – was removed in 1875-6. Inside the church there is a wealth of interest, including a private chapel for the Sandys family, which included a former Archbishop of York, founder of the grammar school in 1585. A primitive dug out chest is of great antiquity.

Also in Hawkshead is the **Beatrix Potter Gallery**, a collection of

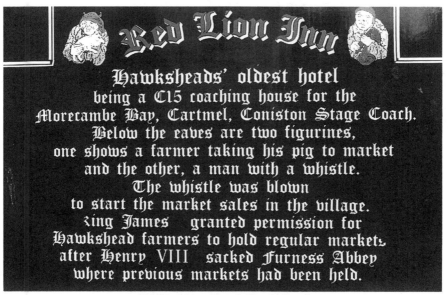

The Red Lion Hotel, Hawkshead

the wonderful original illustrations of her world famous children's books, housed in the building which was formerly the office of her solicitor husband, William Heelis. Owned by the National Trust, the Gallery is open from Easter to the end of October. The Tourist Information Centre is adjacent to the main car park.

At 245m (803ft), **Latterbarrow** hardly challenges the Lakeland giants but it is a nicely shaped little peak, crowned by a well-constructed obelisk, with views well worth the modest effort required for the ascent.

The Walk   ✓ April 2002

From the car park return to the by pass road and turn left. Turn right at a 'public footpath' signpost in 200m or so along a roadway giving access to property. Go to the right to pass by the property, cross Black Beck on a footbridge and turn left.

Angle across a meadow to a waymarked kissing gate and follow the indicated line across the next meadow. After another kissing gate fork left at a 'Loanthwaite' sign and climb gently to join Scar House Lane. Turn left for 40m and then turn right through a kissing gate, rising again, along the edge of a meadow. On approaching a farm, follow the waymarks to reach a minor public road, Loanthwaite Lane.

Turn right, along the road, following a 'Latterbarrow' sign, to a road junction. Turn left along this road for 100m, then turn right at a gate with 'public footpath' sign. A stony track now rises through the National Trust Latterbarrow Estate. Ignore a minor diversion to the left and continue to a more major fork before turning left along a broad grassy track between bracken, heading directly for the summit of Latterbarrow, where there is a well made obelisk.

The views are very good, the Fairfield Horseshoe above Ambleside being particularly prominent. For an enhanced view of Windermere, walk a little further to the north from the summit.

To descend from the obelisk take a track just a little to the left of the upward route, again on grass between the bracken. Rejoin the main path close to a signposted gate, noting a white marker post, part of a marked route across the often confusing Claiffe Heights. Turn left, go over a stile and continue along a well used path through the woodland. As a stone wall is approached the track bends to the right, still following the white topped posts. In a short distance, go

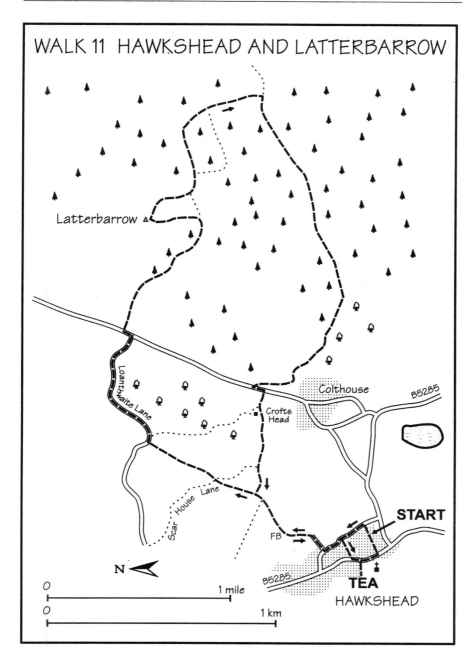

WALK 11 HAWKSHEAD AND LATTERBARROW

Latterbarrow

Loanthwaite Lane

Colthouse

B5285

Crofts Head

Scar House Lane

START

FB

TEA

N

B5285

HAWKSHEAD

0   1 mile

0   1 km

through a gap in the wall on the left and drop steeply down a bank before continuing in much the same direction as before, with a wall on the left.

On reaching a major junction by a gate turn right, through the gate, to follow 'Bridleway, Hawkshead'. This broad track is easy to follow as it heads past two small tarns in the woodland. As more open country is reached, with views over Hawkshead, descend to the right to reach the minor road a little way north of Colthouse.

Turn left along the road for 50m then turn right into the access roadway to Crofts Bank Farm. Turn left at a 'public footpath' sign just before the main house, go to a gate and turn right towards a gap in a wall, as indicated by a white arrow on a stile. Don't go over the stile. After the gap angle left towards a waymark on a post. Continue the same line to a waymarked stile over a stone wall in the bottom corner of the field.

Go down a bank to a gate giving access to Scar House Lane. Go across the lane to take a path signposted 'public footpath, Hawkshead Hall'. Rejoin the outward route by a kissing gate and go left to return to the village.

12. Great Langdale and Lingmoor

Length: 8 miles.

Summary: One of the longer walks in the book, this rewarding circuit takes more time than would be expected from the mileage. The path along the top of Lingmoor ('Heather Moor') 469m. (1539ft), twists and turns incessantly and has rocky sections which need more than usual care. Lingmoor is a great viewpoint for the array of mountains which enclose the head of Langdale – Crinkle Crags, Pike o'Blisco, Bowfell, and the Langdale Pikes. The Coniston group of fells, particularly Wetherlam, are also well seen.

Car Parking: National Trust car park in Elterwater village, with public conveniences adjacent, grid reference 328048. Alternative car park on Elterwater Common, nearby, grid reference 329051

Map: Ordnance Survey Outdoor Leisure no. 6, The English Lakes, south-western area, 1:25,000 or Landranger no. 90, Penrith and Keswick, 1:50,000.

Tea Shop

The Stickle Barn is not our usual type of tea shop. In fact it is not really a tea shop at all; it has the atmosphere of a public house and is actually known as a tavern. Nevertheless it is a welcome sight and an opportunity for refreshments. On offer is a full range of bar type food but also available are coffee, tea, cakes, Danish pastries, etc. This is a great rendezvous for serious and not-so-serious mountaineers – climbing photographs adorn the walls. There is a huge outdoor eating area in a splendid setting towards the head of Great Langdale.

Open: all day every day throughout the year. Tel: 015394 37356

About the Area

Great Langdale has long been a favourite valley, its textbook glacial 'U' shape providing level valley bottom walks, whilst at the same time accentuating the steep rocky sides of the surrounding mountains which are so appealing to the tougher fell walkers. Easy access to motorway and railway to the south east ensures that there is never a shortage of visitors.

There is much of interest within the valley, not least the two old hostelries, the Old and the New Dungeon Ghylls; the latter has the Stickle Barn, our recommended tea shop. Elterwater and Chapel Stile are charming little villages and the popularity of the Brittania Inn at the former is now legendary.

The proximity of the large quarry reminds us that this part of Langdale was, and still is, an industrial centre. The adjacent time-share complex occupies the site of an extensive former gunpowder works, of which traces remain, including the enlarged Stickle Tarn, high up the side of Harrison Stickle.

Lingmoor Fell is a long, partially rocky, ridge, which provides the perfect viewing gallery for its mightier neighbours. The challenging upthrust of Side Pike at the north-western end of the ridge is quite impassable for walkers, who must follow the route below to circumvent this obstacle

Stickle Barn tea shop

The Walk

From either car park go to the road bridge over Gt. Langdale Beck, just past the Brittania Inn. Continue along the road, passing the youth hostel. At the first junction turn right into a surfaced road, uphill. In a short distance turn right into a cul de sac road and pass a house, still rising.

Fork left on to a stony track, signposted ' public bridleway, Little Langdale' and continue uphill, through the woods. Go straight ahead at a junction, soon passing old quarry spoil heaps, now with views over Great Langdale and the working portion of the quarry. After leaving the woodland, look out for a white arrow on a post; turn sharp left here on to a narrower stony track directly up the hillside to a wall and stile at the top.

Go over and turn right, along a grass track between bracken, still rising quite steeply with the wall close on the right. Along this broad ridge the views include Little Langdale, Elterwater and the Coniston group of fells to the left. As the crow flies, the distance to Side Pike at the far end of the ridge is now only about 1¼ miles. For the walker, less fortunate in this respect than the crow, it is much further and over very little of the route can speedy progress be made. So, allow plenty of time and enjoy the views.

The main path along the top is not difficult to follow, although there are occasional diversions, mainly to the right. Be careful here; there are dangerously exposed old quarries in this direction. When the path descends a little to the left and a cross wall is approached, turn back right at two large cairns and climb steeply uphill to the summit, 'Brown Howe' on Ordnance Survey maps. Go over the stile at the top and turn left. The water ahead is Lingmoor Tarn.

Carry on by the side of the wall, soon descending to the left to follow the wall round. Blea Tarn is now in view, with Side Pike obviously blocking the way ahead. Descend to the col and, before the fence, turn left to continue the descent beside the fence. About 100m before the Blea Tarn road, turn right to go over a stile and take a footpath which stays parallel with the road for some distance.

Just after the cross wall, which is at the road summit, the path divides. Continue downhill, close to the wall on the left, heading for the visible Old Dungeon Ghyll Hotel. Reach woodland at a stile. Don't go over, but turn right along a minor footpath to a kissing gate, soon joining a more major path from the left. Go to Side House (farm) and turn left through the farm and along the farm access roadway to join the valley road. Cross over and walk to the Stickle Barn opposite for refreshment (and public conveniences).

Return to the road and cross over to the public car park, turning left to follow the old valley road, now a fine wide footpath. Rejoin the public road and turn right for a short distance, soon turning right again at a 'public bridleway' sign, slightly downhill. A good stony track leads to a footbridge over the beck.

Cross and turn left for half a mile or so along part of the Cumbria Way. Turn left to cross the beck again on the Baysbrown Farm access bridge. Just short of the valley road turn right to pass Thrang Farm and the back of the school before rejoining the valley road.

Turn right, pass the Wainwright's Inn (no – it had nothing to do with the great man!), and turn right again at the end of the Inn car park to cross the beck yet again on a footbridge. Turn left to take the well-made path along the bottom edge of the quarry spoil, with the time share complex across the beck. Rise to join the quarry road, turning left to return to Elterwater.

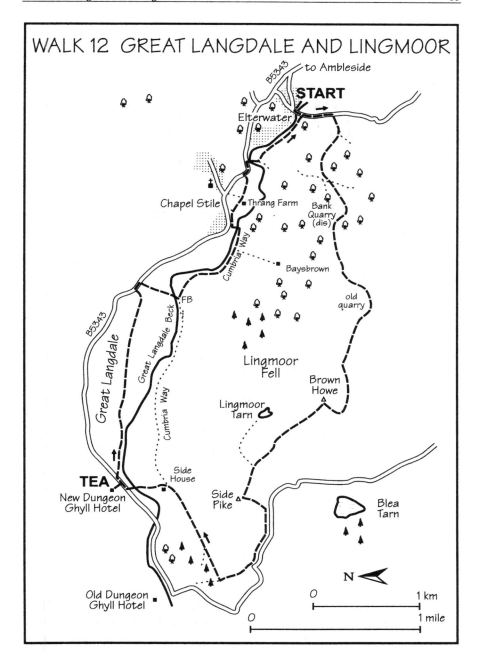

WALK 12 GREAT LANGDALE AND LINGMOOR

to Ambleside

B5343

START

Elterwater

Chapel Stile

Thrang Farm

Bank Quarry (dis)

Cumbria Way

Baysbrown

old quarry

FB

Great Langdale Beck

B5343

Great Langdale

Lingmoor Fell

Brown Howe

Cumbria Way

Lingmoor Tarn

Side House

TEA

New Dungeon Ghyll Hotel

Side Pike

Blea Tarn

Old Dungeon Ghyll Hotel

N

0   1 km

0   1 mile

13. Coniston and Brantwood

Length: 3 miles (longer version 3½ miles)

Summary: A comparatively short walk, largely in part of the extensive Grizedale Forest, is combined with a visit to Brantwood to make an attractive package. The basic route has a steep initial ascent, which can be avoided by using the longer option. Paths are unfailingly good; a little more than one mile is along the quiet minor road by the side of the lake.

Car Parking: Forest Enterprises car park (free) by the roadside approximately half a mile south of Brantwood. Picnic tables and public conveniences (in season only). Grid reference 310952.

Map: Ordnance Survey Outdoor Leisure no.6 or no. 7, The English Lakes, south-western or south-eastern areas, 1:25,000 or Landranger no. 97, Kendal to Morecambe, 1:50,000.

Tea Shop

The Jumping Jenny Tea Room at Brantwood is beautifully situated overlooking Coniston Water – the views from the terrace are quite stunning. The café is in the old stables and the stalls have been retained to form individual seating areas. On cooler days the wood-burning stove is a great attraction. Good selection of food – counter service but on the two occasions we visited the café the service was somewhat slow and the staff appeared to be under pressure, so try not to be short of time. The food is of good quality and the menu includes pasta dishes, home-made soup, open sandwiches, and salads. Excellent scones, home-made cakes, choice of teas, iced tea, coffee, and cold drinks.

Open: 11am to 6pm (4.30pm in winter) every day. From mid-November to mid-March closed every Tuesday. Also closed on Christmas Day. Tel: 015394 41715

About the Area

Although this walk does not actually involve Coniston village, it lies close and many will no doubt wish to visit the small museum (being rebuilt in 1998), Ruskin's grave in the churchyard and other attrac-

SS Gondola at Brantwood jetty, Coniston Water

tions. There is a launch service across Coniston Water, from a jetty close to Brantwood. The ferry operates a timetabled service daily from Easter to the end of October, with a very limited winter service. Tel. 015394 36216.

The most dramatic event in the history of Coniston Water occurred in 1967, when Donald Campbell, who had followed his father, Malcolm, in attempting world water speed records, was killed when his boat somersaulted at 300mph. Much more tranquilly, the steam yacht 'Gondola' plies elegantly around the lake during the normal National Trust season, from Easter or the beginning of April to the end of October. This fine boat was launched on the lake in 1859, operating until it was cannibalised in 1937. During a storm in 1963 the hulk was stranded and left in very poor condition. Following a survey in 1977, the National Trust took over the huge task of restoring Gondola to full Victorian elegance. They were obviously very successful.

The beautifully situated large house, **Brantwood**, was the home of the great poet, social reformer, artist and philosopher John Ruskin (1819 – 1900) from 1872 until his death. Many of his drawings and watercolours are hung in the house and there are also a video programme, bookshop and the Coach House Gallery, with an array of crafts. Extensive gardens provide pleasant walks. There are periodic displays of the making of Ruskin lace and occasional theatrical events. House and gardens are open to the public all year, mid March to mid November from 1100 to 1730, in winter from Wednesday to Sunday, 1100 to 1600. There is more restricted opening of the Coach House Gallery. Tel. 015394 41396.

The Walk

Leave the car park by the signposted 'purple walk, 1.5 miles', an obvious path soon climbing quite steeply, fairly close to a tumbling stream. The route is marked by posts with a purple band. A section has been improved by the provision of rudimentary steps and handrails.

Join a broader track and turn right, uphill, to a stile. Continue through mixed woodland, including beech, which hardly looks like managed commercial forest. The gradient eases before the stream is crossed. Twenty metres after the stream leave the 'purple route' by turning left up a wheel rutted track. Go through a wide gap in a wall and join a wide access roadway.

Turn left to follow the roadway, rising gently towards Lawson Park. At a point where two roadways join, the Ordnance Survey maps show a viewpoint. More recent planting has, alas, much diminished the views of Coniston Water and the Coniston group of fells.

Go straight on to reach the old farmstead of Lawson Park, now apparently in some kind of rather basic holiday/leisure use. This is the highest part of the walk and the views really are there – the lake and the group of fells including Coniston Old Man, Swirl How and Wetherlam.

After Lawson Park, bear left to start the descent along a waymarked bridleway, initially through open country, with continuing views. Cross a railway sleeper bridge and continue to a most un-

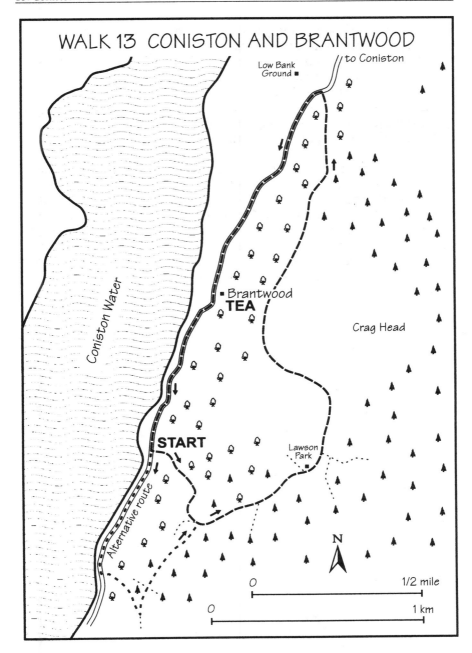

WALK 13 CONISTON AND BRANTWOOD

to Coniston

Low Bank Ground ■

Brantwood
TEA

Crag Head

Coniston Water

START

Lawson Park

Alternative route

N

0   1/2 mile

0   1 km

usual 'S' shaped seat, facing two directions. Enter woodland here, with silver birch dominant. There is a trail with white marked numbered posts sharing our route for some distance. Ignore this and stay with the excellent path as it descends gently, crossing several becks, which are culverted below.

The public road is reached at a gate. Turn left to walk along the quiet road for a little more than half a mile to Brantwood. Coniston village, with the Copper Mines Valley behind, is well seen across the water.

Leave Brantwood by continuing along the road for a further half a mile, largely along the side of the lake, to return to the car park.

For the alternative start to the walk, head south along the road for rather less than half a mile. Turn left just beyond a pair of concrete (Airey) houses into a broad roadway, the access to Lawson Park. By angling its route and with a very sharp left hand bend, this roadway gains the necessary height at a much gentler gradient than the footpath. The two routes come together close to the stream above the car park.

14. Muncaster Fell and Ravenglass

Length: 6 miles

Summary: The long top of Muncaster Fell makes a fine linear ramble among rock, gorse and heather and, it must be said, some bog, with an otherwise splendid path underfoot. Views ahead are to the estuary and the sea, with fine mountain panoply behind. The fell has such a presence that it comes as a surprise to find that its highest point is at a modest 231m. (758ft). It follows that the ascent, spread over a long distance from Eskdale Green station, is not excessive, nor are there steep gradients. The recommended return is by the Ravenglass and Eskdale railway, a delightful 25 minute ride from Ravenglass to Eskdale Green.

Car Parking: Small car park for rail users at Eskdale Green station. No public conveniences. Grid reference 145998.

Map: Ordnance Survey Outdoor Leisure no. 6, The English Lakes, south-western area, 1:25,000 or Landranger no. 96, Barrow in Furness and South Lakes area, 1:50,000.

Tea Shop

The Station Tea Bar at Ravenglass is a basic clean facility with friendly informal service. Usual choice of tea, coffee, scones, sandwiches, and cakes. Hot snacks are also available. From the café it is interesting to watch the bustle on the station with the trains arriving and departing. The ceiling of the tea room is unique; it is completely covered in themed tea towels – perhaps someone's own collection being displayed. Some tables and benches on the platform for warmer days.

Open: Easter to end of October 10.30am to 4pm every day and later in high season when the time-table is more extensive. Tel: 01229 717171

About the Area

More than 3½ miles long, but comparatively narrow, Muncaster Fell separates lower Eskdale from the flatlands drained by the more minor River Mite and from the line of the railway. Close to the start of this walk is Eskdale Green, most important village of the whole valley, with inns and two railway stations among its facilities.

Ravenglass is a former port dating back to at least Roman times, situated between fell and sea at the point where the rivers Esk, Irt and Mite come together to form a great sandy estuary. The only street in the village heads straight down to the estuary, with high tides lapping the end of the tarmac. One or two shops and an inn comprise the facilities; main line and Ravenglass and Eskdale stations are conveniently side by side. Close by are the remains of the Roman fort of Glannoventa, with the bath house walls surviving as probably the highest above ground Roman stonework in the country.

Between Ravenglass and the fell, **Muncaster Castle**, a former defensive pele tower now a major visitor attraction has been the home of the Pennington family for an amazing nearly 800 years. The house has close associations with King Henry VI, who was helped here by Sir John Pennington after his defeat in battle at Hexham in 1464. In gratitude Henry gave a glass bowl, the 'luck' of Muncaster. According to legend the family will prosper so long as the 'luck' remains intact. A replica is on display. The castle can be visited, as can an owl centre and extensive gardens, rich in rhododendrons, camellias and many other fine plants. A plant centre sells direct to the public. Inside the castle grounds is the parish church of St Michael, believed to have survived largely from the 12th century and with fragments of Saxon crosses in the churchyard.

The **Whitehaven and Furness Junction Railway** (later part of the Furness Railway) was opened to Ravenglass in 1849. A rather sparse passenger service runs north to Whitehaven, Workington and Carlisle and south to Barrow in Furness. Beside this station is the terminus and headquarters of the **Ravenglass and Eskdale Railway**, the famous La'al Ratty, the narrow gauge line which runs for more than 7 miles through lovely countryside to Dalegarth, in Eskdale. Originally of 3ft gauge and constructed for iron ore traffic, the railway deteriorated as the iron ore ran out and the subsequent stone quarrying was an insufficient replacement, the line being closed in 1908. Relaid to the present 15" gauge, it was soon re-opened and has become a considerable visitor attraction, heavily used in season and with some reduced services through the winter. The beautifully maintained colourful little locomotives are particularly highly regarded.

The first station out of Ravenglass is at **Muncaster Mill**, a restored

Ravenglass, the estuary

water powered corn mill which is in regular use. Freshly milled products are on sale to visitors, daily from April to October.

The Walk

From Eskdale Green station car park walk back towards the public road and turn right immediately before the road along a lane sign-posted 'public bridleway, Muncaster Head. Muncaster Fell'. In about 150m, before reaching the railway line, fork left along a lane between stone walls.

Go over a stile beside a stream, then cross the stream on stones. Keep to the right of the rising field, close to the wall and woodland. Follow close to the wall, keeping the same general line as the wall turns away to the right. Muncaster Head Farm is below, left, as the not very distinct track stays above a low bank, through a cattle churned area, heading for a wall ahead.

Join a more major route here, turning right, through a gate at an ' Irton Road. Eskdale Green' sign. In 30m turn left up a well-defined path at a yellow waymark to start the climb of Muncaster Fell. Continue uphill to a kissing gate and an excellent path angling up the hillside. Apart from one or two boggy areas, this route along the fell is always easy to follow, in places marked by standing stones.

Before long there is a first view of the sea. Go through a gap in a wall; the top seen ahead is not the summit of the fell, which lies almost one mile away. Less than 100m beyond the wall is an unpleasant bog, where the track appears to veer right. Keep to the left of the bog, where one of the marker stones can just about be seen. As the track forks, keep left to by-pass the minor summit and reach a dolmen-like construction, according to A. Wainwright erected by a shooting party anxious to show off their combined strength by lifting the large capping stone. It is inscribed 'Ross's Camp 1883'.

There are now good views of the generally wet low-lying part of Lower Eskdale, with the river meandering as if reluctant to reach the estuary. The true summit, Hooker Crag, is now in view. Cross another bog with the help of a few stones, heading towards the summit. At a fork, go left to by-pass or right to the top. The top is recommended despite a steep little climb; the views are entirely worthwhile. Ahead is a bird's eye view of the estuary; behind is the great ring of mountains forming the head of Eskdale – Scafell, Esk Pike, Bowfell, the Crinkle Crags with Harter Fell on their right. On the horizon is the Coniston group of fells. On a clear day the Isle of Man can be seen.

Leave the top along the obvious path heading down between plantations; the official route is close to the wood on the right. Go through a kissing gate and continue gently downhill along a broad rhododendron-fringed track. Keep straight on, crossing over the culverted outlet stream from a nearby tarn. In a few metres there is a gate on the right. This may well lead to private land, but there is no warning and there are seats by the side of the tarn, which is reached in a short distance. You may or may not wish to try this diversion.

The main track soon becomes Fell Lane, going straight down to the main A595 road. Turn left to walk along the roadside pavement for a little more than 300m. Turn right at a 'footpath. Ravenglass' signpost, cross the road and enter the Muncaster Castle grounds. Pass St Michael's Church and the plant centre to reach the main area in front of the house, glimpsed through the trees.

WALK 14 ESKDALE, MUNCASTER AND RAVENGLASS

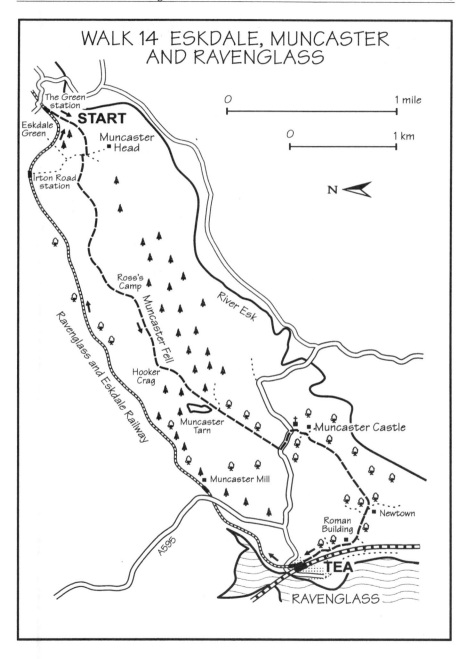

The Green station

START

Eskdale Green

Muncaster Head

Irton Road station

Ross's Camp

Muncaster Fell

River Esk

Ravenglass and Eskdale Railway

Hooker Crag

Muncaster Tarn

Muncaster Castle

Muncaster Mill

Newtown

Roman Building

A595

TEA

RAVENGLASS

0   1 mile

0   1 km

N

Turn right, then left at a footpath sign, to cross the grass by the side of a pond, passing Herman's tortoise. Join a drive and turn left. In 40m fork right, uphill, at a 'Ravenglass via Newton' sign, to rise steadily on a path marked with yellow-topped posts through the lovely gardens.

Exit by a kissing gate in a wall at the top and bear left across a huge descending meadow on the line indicated by the signpost. At first the path is indistinct; aim for a large boulder, then pick up a line of yellow-topped posts, at least some of which may well be lying on the ground. Aim for a stile now visible at the top of a plantation, now on a more worn path.

Go over the stile and descend on a good path through the plantation. Join an unsurfaced roadway at a little gate and turn right. Ignore a right turn, join a surfaced road and bear right to reach the Roman bath house. A short distance after passing paths which join the road on each side, go left between the trees to follow a well-used path along the edge of a meadow, aiming for the footbridge over the railway and the station beyond.

15. Gosforth

Length:	4¼ miles.
Summary:	A straightforward walk through attractive countryside on good paths, with views to the mountains and over the sea from the higher part of the route. The ascent from Gosforth is about 135m (443ft) in total. About 1¼ miles is by the side of very minor roads.
Car Parking:	Free car park with public conveniences in Gosforth village. Grid reference 068036.
Map:	Ordnance Survey Outdoor Leisure no. 6, The English Lakes, south-western area, 1:25,000 or Landranger no. 89, West Cumbria, 1:50,000

Tea Shop

The Mill Race Tea room at Walkmill Garden Centre is one our "surprise" finds. Access to the café is through the garden centre – always of interest – can one fit some plants into the rucksack for remainder of the walk? Decor is in character with the setting – fresh looking white furniture and plants. Counter service for tea, iced tea, coffee (milky, cafétière, decaffeinated), hot chocolate, and cold drinks. Food available includes quiche, toasted sandwiches, scones, and delectable cakes. Prices are particularly reasonable.

Open: 9am to 5pm daily except Sunday when open 11pm to 5pm. Close earlier daily in winter month Tel: 019467 25293

About the Area

Gosforth is an attractive village on the western fringe of the Lake District, just off the main A595 Barrow to Whitehaven road and barely three miles from the coast at Seascale. As with most of the Cumbria coast, the remoteness from centres of population keeps Gosforth comparatively quiet, although the major visitor attraction of Sellafield, the nuclear reprocessing plant, is only three miles away. The village is well provided with shops, including an excellent home bakery.

In St Mary's churchyard is the **Gosforth cross**, a 'Viking' monument of national importance, dating from the latter part of the 10th century. This slender column, more than 14ft in height, is the tallest

Gosforth Cross

surviving ancient cross in Britain. Most intriguing is the mixture of Christian and earlier Norse pagan beliefs depicted by the carving. It has been suggested, a little tongue in cheek, that this might indicate an each-way bet on the afterlife by the sculptor! Explanatory leaflets are available in the church. Inside the church are other Norse fragments including two particularly good 'hogback' tombstones, each representing a house with steep pitched roof, with pictorial carving. 'Hogback' stones were placed over graves after the influx of Norse colonisers in the 10th century.

The Walk

Walk along the village street, away from the direction of the main A595 road. Fork left as the road divides, soon reaching St Mary's church. Turn left just before the church at a 'public footpath' sign, heading towards the Gosforth Hall Hotel. Pass between the hotel and a large sandstone building, then the hotel reception, to a waymarked gate.

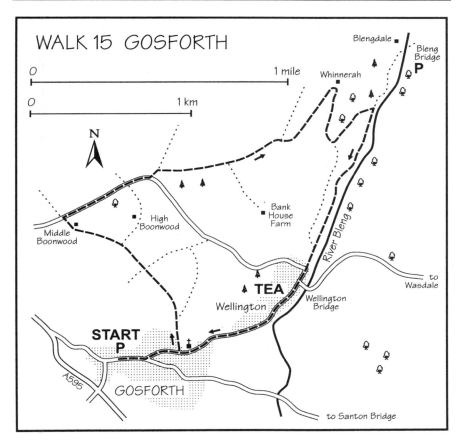

After passing a few dwellings and another gate, go across a large rising field; the path is rather indistinct but head for a waymarked stile close to the top left corner. After the stile bear left and stay close to the boundary to reach a farm gate, with paths to left and right.

Go through the gate and straight on along an unsurfaced lane. At the far end of the lane pass through Middle Boonwood Farm to join a minor public road, nothing more than a lane, with wide grassy verge. Turn right, then in less than half a mile turn left at a junction.

Turn right in 40m, after the road has lost its surface, at a 'Bank House Park, Whinnerah' signpost. An unsurfaced lane rises gently, with a coniferous plantation on the right. Scafell and Scafell Pikes are in view, ahead, and right. In less than half a mile fork right, down the entrance drive to Whinnerah (farm).

By the entrance to the farm turn right, over a stile, and descend for 30m beside the fence, then turning right to follow an attractive terraced path diagonally descending the side of the valley of the River Bleng. Pass an old wall and then turn sharp left to rake back by the side of a wall, still descending. Enter woodland and continue to a gate. Go through and join a private road, now quite close to the river.

Turn right and walk along the valley bottom to a public road, going straight on and passing scattered dwellings before reaching a road junction signposted 'Gosforth 1', with Wellington Bridge to the left. Go straight on; the entrance to the garden centre and the Millrace coffee house is about 150m, on the right.

From the garden centre continue along the road to Gosforth, just over half a mile distant.

16. Buttermere and Red Pike

Length: 5 miles

Summary: Don't be misled by the apparently short length of this walk. The ascent
of Red Pike from Buttermere involves a long, steep, climb to the 755m
(2478ft) high summit. Much of the circuit has rough, stony, paths,
particularly along the side of Scales Beck, where there are one or two
mini scrambles. Having said that, for those who like high places with
wonderful views, this is a fine walk with the bonus of visiting Scale
Force, Lakeland's highest waterfall.

Car Parking: Car park (pay in season) with public conveniences by the side of the
Fish Inn, Buttermere village. Grid reference 175169.

Map: Ordnance Survey Outdoor Leisure no. 4, The English Lakes, north-
western area, 1:25,000 or Landranger no. 89, West Cumbria, 1:50,000

Tea Shop

Croft House, in the heart of Buttermere hamlet, is a 'no frills' traditional walkers' tea shop serving tea (mugs or cups) coffee and cold
drinks. Food is limited to filled rolls, crisps, cakes, biscuits and ice
cream. Inside, the tea shop is clean and spacious, with plenty of
room for rucksacks. With stunning views of Red Pike and Sour Milk
Ghyll the outside tables are understandably popular.
Open: 10.30am to 5.30pm from Good Friday to end of October but
closed on Saturdays. Tel: 017687 70235

About the Area

The beautiful valley of Buttermere and Crummock Water, with its
tributary which contains Loweswater, is one of the finest in the Lake
District, a must for inclusion in any walking guide. Fortunately
there is a conveniently located tea shop which combines well with
the circuit set out below.

   The valley is readily reached from Borrowdale over the Honister
Pass, from Keswick either by Newlands Hause or the Whinlatter
Pass and, easiest route of all, from Cockermouth via the Vale of Lor-
ton. Although high, none of these passes poses any real difficulty.

   Several thousand years ago most of the valley was filled by one
huge lake but the progressive deposition of silt by streams such as

Buttermere: Croft House Café

Sour Milk Gill and Mill Beck has produced the strip of alluvial land which now separates Buttermere from Crummock Water. Red Pike is just one peak on the ridge which also includes High Stile and High Crag before the drop to the Scarth Gap Pass and the following rise to the lesser height of Haystacks. The latter was a great favourite of the late and legendary hill walker/writer A. Wainwright; his ashes were scattered near Innominate Tarn, close to the summit. At the head of the valley is the elegant shape of Fleetwith Pike, with the bulk of Honister Crag towering over the top of the pass. Geologically, Red Pike is part of a granitic intrusion into the prevailing Borrowdale Series of volcanic rocks. The name is very obviously derived from the ruddy colour of the rocks and the even more ruddy eroded shale.

Buttermere village has a well-sited little church, with a tasteful memorial to Wainwright sited below a window which looks across to Haystacks, two inns and the essential tea shop.

The Walk

Walk round the front of the Fish Hotel, keeping right to take a broad track between fences, heading straight across the valley. Keep left as the track forks, go through a kissing gate, and fork right, now close to the lake and heading directly towards the prominent Sour Milk Gill, rushing down the steep hillside in great leaps and bounds.

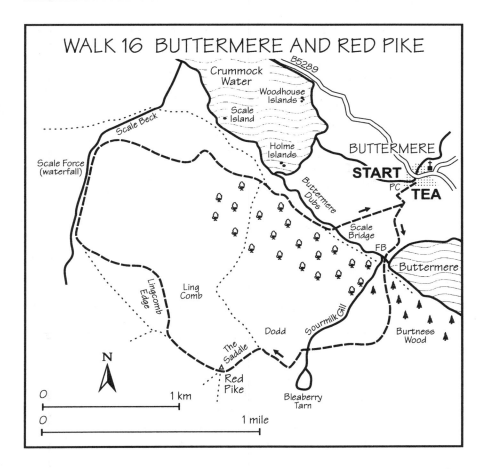

WALK 16 BUTTERMERE AND RED PIKE

Go ahead to a small bridge over the gill and through a gate on the right to start the ascent on an engineered path, part of the erosion control which is very much a feature of this route.

The path rises steadily through Burtness Wood, largely larch, with some silver birch towards the top, soon reaching open hillside, bearing to the left. Go through a gate in a fence and continue along a natural path, clearly defined as it bends to the right. The views across the valley are over Buttermere village to Whiteless Pike and the rather bland side of the Robinson, Hindscarth, Dale Head group of fells. Fleetwith Pike closes the head of the valley.

The colour of the rock and shale leaves no doubt as to the origin of the Red Pike name. After another engineered section, a series of cairns leads to the upper part of Sour Milk Gill and into the hanging valley (corrie) containing Bleaberry Tarn, quite a little jewel. Bear right here to climb to the Saddle, a high col linking the subsidiary top of Dodd to the main mountain. Turn left for the final section, a struggle up loose shale to reach the summit.

The splendid views include Skiddaw, Blencathra, Helvellyn, Scafell, Scafell Pikes, a host of lesser fells and five major lakes.

Continue from the summit in a north-easterly direction, initially descending steeply among rocks, with cairns. In a few metres the path forks; keep right here and follow the path which goes along the top of Langcombe Edge, a fine scarp to the right. Ahead, the bulk of Melbreak separates Loweswater from Crummock Water. The stony path is clear as it bends to the left to reach Scale Beck, well above the falls.

The path now keeps close to the stream, largely over rocky ground, quite awkward in places. Descend to the bridge below the falls and divert upstream for a few metres for the best viewing position. Return without crossing the stream to go through a gap in a wall on a short section of man-made path.

Continue round the flank of Blea Crag, following cairns towards Buttermere village. For some distance the path is uncomfortably stony, keeping above the wet ground closer to the lake. In approximately half a mile from the fall, turn left to follow the cairns down towards the lake. In about 200m, just below a large cairn, join another path and turn right. The way is now straightforward, soon close to Buttermere Dubs, the river connecting the two lakes. Turn left over Scale Bridge and take the broad easy track back to the village.

17. Whinlatter and Lord's Seat

Length:	5 miles.
Summary:	A fine walk combining Thornthwaite Forest with the adjacent summits of Lord's Seat, 552m (1811ft) and Barf, 468m (1536ft). Apart from a swampy area in the depression between the two mountain tops, the tracks are extremely good throughout. A fair amount of ascent, but all at easy gradients. Splendid views.
Car Parking:	Pay and display at Whinlatter Visitor Centre, easily found along the Braithwaite to Lorton road, on the Keswick side of the top of the Whinlatter Pass. Grid reference 208245.
Map:	Ordnance Survey Outdoor Leisure no. 4, The English Lakes, north-western area, 1:25,000 or Landranger no. 89, West Cumbria, 1:50,000. The Visitor Centre has a most useful Forest Enterprises 'Guide to the Forest Park' map at 1:20,000, with plenty of ancillary information.

Tea Shop

The café at Whinlatter Visitor Centre is in a beautiful setting and the building is sympathetic to its environment in the forest. Even the names on the menu are evocative of the area with such dishes as "wood cutters' soup" – home-made vegetable, "Noble Knott Pasta", "tree-top toasties" and many other choices. Drinks include, tea – Lakeland Special, Assam, Earl Grey, and others. Good coffee is served. Wicked but delicious is the hot chocolate served topped with whipped cream and a chocolate flake. Cold drinks include elderflower cordial. For something more unusual try the hot Lakeland punch, a non-alcoholic drink especially welcome on cold days.

Open: 10am to 5pm everyday but closes at 4pm in the winter months except at busy periods such as school holidays. Tel: 017687 78068

About the Area

Whinlatter Forest Park claims to be 'England's only mountain forest'. Unlike some Lake District commercial forests, Whinlatter is quite diverse, spread over both sides of the road which climbs over the Whinlatter Pass. As there are considerable open areas and steep slopes, the views are better than is normally expected in a forest.

There are numerous forest roadways, with numbered posts at junctions and designated circuits colour waymarked; the whole area is walker-friendly.

The Visitor Centre is comprehensive, with interpretative displays, shop, catering, and good facilities for children.

Although of quite modest height, Lord's Seat and Barf are real mountains with open, wind-swept, tops and fine views. From Barf the view over Bassenthwaite Lake to Skiddaw and its outliers is particularly good. Lord's Seat has the commanding position as the highest point at the centre of an extensive upland area, Barf being merely an abrupt end to a long broad ridge.

Whinlatter Visitor Centre

The Walk

From the visitor centre car park start uphill, with the visitor centre buildings on the right, following a well-stoned footpath with a 'trails' signpost. Pass a marker post with red, blue and green circular markings. Our first destination is Horsebox Crossroads; the green marker is the one to follow. Stay with the main forest trail, uphill, to

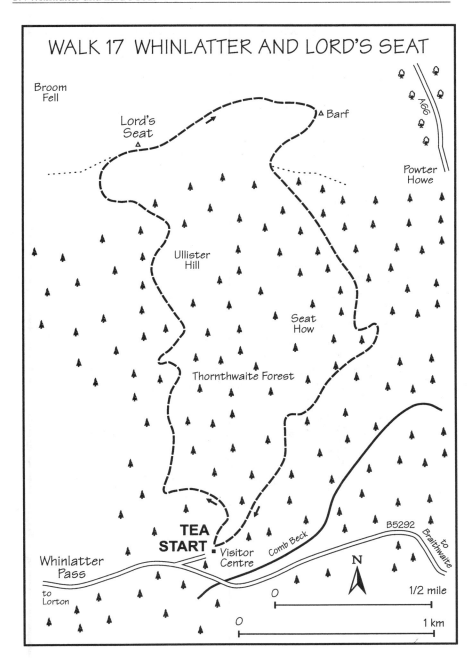

WALK 17 WHINLATTER AND LORD'S SEAT

Broom
Fell

Lord's
Seat

Barf

Powter
Howe

A66

Ullister
Hill

Seat
How

Thornthwaite Forest

TEA
START

Whinlatter
Pass

Visitor
Centre

Comb Beck

B5292

to
Braithwaite

to
Lorton

N

0   1/2 mile

0   1 km

reach a large clearing with helpful view boards and rudimentary seats.

Turn left here to follow a path with green banded posts, uphill. Join a broad forest roadway and turn left to reach Horsebox Crossroads, at marker post no. 2. This is a viewpoint for Grisedale Pike. Follow the arrows to the right to continue along a broad trail, steadily uphill.

The next large clearing is at marker post 3. Turn right here along another forest trail, level for some distance. Go left at a fork and along a terraced section, across the slope of Ullister Hill. Continue to rise across more open, heather-clad ground, to marker post 5. Turn left here, to take a good footpath across a boggy area. At post 6 keep to the main path, bearing left, uphill

At post 23, go over a stile and take the fairly obvious path to the summit of Lord's Seat. On a clear day the southern Scottish hills can be seen over the Solway Firth.

Continue along the broad, grassy, top, through a swampy area in a depression, before rising, steeply over the final few metres, to the summit of Barf.

Leave Barf by the main track, to the right, and descend to Beckstones Gill. Cross and re-enter the forest at a stile, bearing left, downhill, to post 21. Stay with the forest roadway, rising slightly. Carry on downhill at post 8. This must be one of the most attractive tracks in the whole of the forest, with the Vale of Keswick below, deep among the surrounding mountains.

Turn sharp left at post 9 to continue downhill to post 11. Go diagonally across another roadway to descend a steeper, stony, footpath. Go over Comb Gill and bear left. Don't go down the steps, but take the broad footpath adjacent, slightly downhill. At post 13 fork right, uphill, and proceed straight on past post 14 to return to the Visitor Centre.

18. Bassenthwaite

Length: 5½ miles

Summary: An attractive circuit based on Bassenthwaite village, with just a little initial ascent on a quiet road, followed by a terraced path with long views, woodland, and a return close to the shore of Bassenthwaite Lake. Apart from some mud in wet weather, very good underfoot. A modest distance on roads and roadsides, mostly very quiet.

Car Parking: There are several informal parking spaces in Bassenthwaite village. On the north side of Halls Beck by the bridge, grid reference 231324 is as good as any.

Map: Ordnance Survey Pathfinder no.576, Caldbeck, 1:25,000 or Landranger no. 89, West Cumbria, 1:50,000.

Lambing time: Bassenthwaite

Tea Shop

Trotters, an animal farm park, is not a traditional tea shop but a large café at a tourist attraction. However it is an interesting place to have some refreshment part of the way round the walk, especially if walking with children, as it is possible to watch some of the animals from the windows of the café. Everything is served here from tea and cakes to burger and chips!

Open: Easter to end of October 10am to 5pm. Remainder of the year on Saturdays and Sundays only 11am to 3.30pm. Tel: 01768776239

About the Area

Bassenthwaite village is small and off the beaten track, accessed only by minor roads and hardly affected by tourism. Although the Green is a little disappointing, there is an inn and some good old houses; Halls Beck hurries attractively along one edge of the village.

Bassenthwaite Lake is huge and on its far side the steep slopes of Sale Fell, Barf and Seat Howe form a continuous wall towering above the water with the major road, A66, squeezed along the lake shore. To the south-east of Bassenthwaite the huge bulk of Skiddaw and its offshoot Ullock Pike are quite superb.

The Walk

From the recommended car park at the bridge by the inn, turn left and then right to start the ascent up a minor road, signposted 'Robin Hood', soon passing Hill Farm. This road is called 'The Rake'; initially the gradient is fairly steep and there are soon views back to Skiddaw and across the lake.

As the road bends right, turn left through a gate with two 'public footpath' signs. Keep right, along a fine grassy track near the fence, with gallery-like views. After a 'permissive footpath' sign continue through a gate and along the top edge of mixed woodland (Bank Wood). Pass above disused quarries; the gentle hill away to the right is Binsey.

Turn left, downhill, zig-zagging to regain the previous line of direction, now amongst rhododendrons and holly. As the path appears to veer away to the left, look carefully for a turn to the right, under large bushes, leading shortly to a large, partly mock-Tudor, building. This former hotel is now the Bassenfell Manor Christian

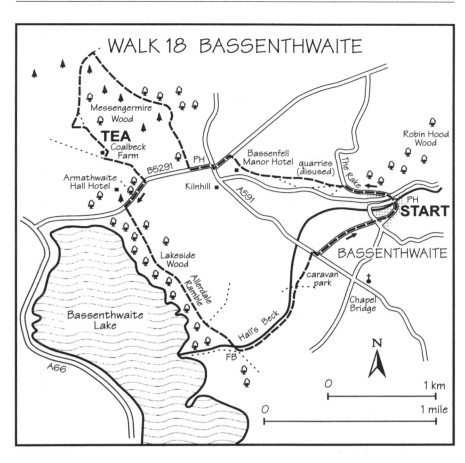

Centre. Go right to pass through the car park behind the Centre (this part of the route is still on a permissive basis) and continue along a surfaced access drive, bearing left at a junction. Join the public road and turn left.

In 200m go straight across at the Castle Inn road junction and then follow the roadside verge for a further 200m. Turn right into a surfaced roadway at a 'public bridleway Irton House and Bewaldeth' sign. After passing a Cumbria Contracting depot, the roadway progressively loses its surface. Cross Coal Beck at the near edge of Messengermire Wood (Forest Enterprise) and bear right to follow the bridleway into the wood.

The path rises gently among the gorse, some of which is too close for comfort, particularly for wearers of shorts, and is rather horse-churned in places. The woodland is mainly silver birch, with primroses lining the way in spring. Go through a small gate at the top of the wood. There is little sign of a path across the meadow in front; the Ordnance Survey shows the right of way aiming a little to the right of the ruined building, Lingeybank, ahead. Find the least cattle-churned route.

Turn left on reaching a wide, stoned, track on the far side of the meadow, go through or over a gate/stile and descend by the side of Lingeybank wood. Go straight across a forest trackway, following a ' public footpath Coalbeck Farm' signpost. At another gate/stile take a track heading towards a farm building, with Messengermire Wood close on the left.

At a gate, the right of way goes over a stile on the left, then diagonally across a field. In view of the 'Keep out – bull' notice, walkers with no desire to become impromptu matadors are recommended to stay with the roadway as far as the farm buildings, turning left there to continue direct to Coalbeck Farm. On the right, the fields house some of the varied and unusual animals of Trotters farm animal park. At the farm are the entrance to the animal collection, an equestrian centre, and the tea shop.

To leave Trotters, go along the access road and turn left to walk to the public road, passing the Coalbeck Farm Static Caravan Park. Turn right along the road side for a little more than 300m. Turn left at a gate just before an overbridge; the signpost reads 'footpath Scarness 1¼ miles'.

Part of Allerdale Ramble, the path is initially muddy but soon improves. Helped by many stiles and the odd plank bridge it stays by the side of Lakeside Wood, roughly parallel with the lake shore. It is generally clear on the close grazed grass of several meadows. At one point there is a short woodland traverse, largely on board walkways over richly vegetated swamp and through a carpet of wood anemones.

At the far end of this woodland go over a waymarked stile and turn left for 50m, then right over two stiles, in a short distance crossing a minor beck before turning left. Cross a major stream, Halls Beck, on a footbridge, then turn left to follow a good path along the beck side. Cross over again on another footbridge by the confluence with Chapel Beck.

After a stile, cross a meadow, bearing left to another stile, still by the side of the beck. Continue close to the beck to a stile giving access to a lane, which can be seriously muddy in wet weather. Turn right to head for the caravan site and the public road, A591, turning right at the road for 40m. The caravan site has a shop open to the public and there is a petrol filling station a few metres further along the road.

Before the filling station, turn left to follow a quiet lane back to Bassenthwaite village, passing the Methodist Chapel, the Green and the Inn.

19. Portinscale, Thornthwaite and Braithwaite

Length: 6¼ miles

Summary: A low level walk without serious ascent linking three of the villages situated to the west of Keswick. The outward route is across the alluvial land between Derwentwater and Bassenthwaite Lake, low lying and a little muddy in wet weather. Some lengths of path are not well defined. The return is on very good tracks, part way up the hillside behind Thornthwaite and Braithwaite, with a short section of very quiet public road.

Car Parking: In Portinscale village. From the main A66, Penrith to Cockermouth road, turn into the village and then turn left at the main village junction. Roadside parking is possible along one side as this cul de sac widens. There is a turning circle at the end. Grid reference 253237.

Map: Ordnance Survey Outdoor Leisure no. 4, The English Lakes, north-western area, 1:25,000 or Landranger no. 90, Penrith and Keswick, 1:50,000.

Tea Shop

Thornthwaite Gallery is a smart venue but, subject to leaving boots and rucksacks by the door, walkers are welcome. The Gallery displays of art, sculpture, jewellery, and pottery are of good quality, beautifully designed, and can prove irresistible.

The café area seats just eighteen people. It is purely a tea shop offering a limited range of food and drink including toasted muffins, tea cakes, pastries, cakes, tea, coffee, hot chocolate, and cold drinks. Try the banana cake – it is delicious.

Open: February to end of December 10.30am to 4.30pm but closed on Tuesdays. Out of main season, to avoid disappointment, suggest telephoning first. Tel: 017687 78248 or 01946 861018

About the Area

Only a few thousand years ago Derwentwater and Bassenthwaite were one huge lake. The progressive deposit of silt by several water-

Suspension bridge at Portinscale

courses has resulted in a three mile strip of alluvial land, which now separates the two lakes. Inevitably this land is low lying and much of it is of very low agricultural value. The River Derwent and various becks are artificially channelled to prevent flooding; names such as Rough Mire, Braithwaite Moss and Bog House are very indicative.

Along the fringe of this area, at the foot of the hills and just above flood plain level, a string of villages has developed over the centuries. Portinscale, Braithwaite and Thornthwaite all have a nucleus of old property commensurate with their farming origins, with more modern development being superimposed, as they have become popular living places.

St Mary's Church at Thornthwaite is on the site of an older chapel, which served the village for many years, but it was not until 1836 that burials were permitted. The present structure is mid 19th century and, although of no particular distinction, it does seem absolutely right in its proportioning and for its site. Inside is a fine Harrison organ of 1890.

Quite apart from its use for refreshment, the **Gallery at Thornthwaite** will be of interest to most visitors. Many might wish that they had left credit cards and cheque books behind.

The combination of lanes and footpaths set out below gives the opportunity to visit these three attractive villages within the compass of a walk of modest length.

The Walk

Go towards the shapely little suspension bridge, which crosses the River Derwent at the end of the road and turn left through a gate before the bridge to follow the obvious footpath along the river bank. Rise steeply to a stile and cross the Keswick road to another, signposted, stile. Descend back to the river and continue along the bank. The view to the north is dominated by the Skiddaw group of fells.

Go under the main A66 road, soon reaching the former railway line, with its sadly dismantled bridge over the river. In about 20m fork left across a meadow, aiming for the left hand boundary of the house ahead, where there is a signpost. Cross the access road and go through the signposted gate opposite. The route across the next meadow is just about visible on the ground as it descends to a stile in the bottom, close to the railway embankment.

Cross a stream on a wooden bridge and turn right to stay close to

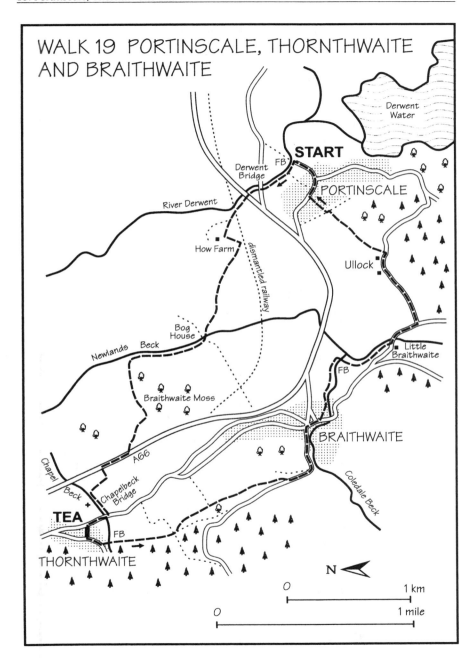

the stream for some distance. To the right is How Farm; the obvious wooded hill is Dodd. Opposite a waymarked post turn left, cross a ditch, then a footbridge. The fells of the north-western group are now very much in view, including Barf with its famous 'Bishop' (a large, white-painted rock).

The access roadway to Bog House is reached, close to a stile/gate. Follow this roadway towards the farm. Just before the farm turn left over a gated footbridge to cross Newlands Beck and turn right immediately, at a 'Thornthwaite' signpost. The path now follows the raised bank of the beck, heavily flood protected across this low-lying area.

After a little less than half a mile, turn left down a few steps by a waymarked post, into a meadow. At first the path is not obvious, but turn right for about 50m and then bear left to a waymarked and worn track. Go through a gate/stile and towards a post with white cap and then over a bridge. Cross a watercourse on another gated footbridge with waymark and continue along a farm track to a junction, where there is a bridge on the left.

Turn right here, along a cattle-churned track. As this becomes indistinct, continue the same line before bearing left to a stile, about 120m from the junction. Cross a flat meadow on a just visible track to reach the main road at a gate/stile by a 'P' sign. Cross the road and turn right, following a 'Public footpath Thornthwaite' sign, initially on the roadside embankment.

Go over a stile on the left and keep close to the hedge on the right. Turn right at a waymarked gate and head for the church. From the church there is a choice: either go through a kissing gate and take a path, with Chapel Beck on the right, or continue along the church access driveway. From the path turn right along the Thornthwaite road, then left up the signposted road to the Thornthwaite Gallery; from the church access go straight across the road.

The gallery is on the right.

After refreshment, put on your boots and take the rising little road, which is ahead as you leave the car park. At a fork go left; the road soon loses its surface. Cross Combe/Chapel Beck; the house on the right has the appearance of having been a water mill. The excellent track is sufficiently elevated to provide views across the broad Keswick Vale.

At a junction go ahead to a kissing gate and a 'public footpath' signpost. A good path runs along the bottom edge of woodland, passing behind the little hill of Braithwaite How to Hope Memorial Camp before joining a public road. Turn left to descend to Braithwaite.

In the village, which has a general store, fork right, then turn right just after the Ivy House Hotel. Turn left immediately before the bridge over Coledale Beck, along a road signposted 'Keswick 2½'. In about 50m turn right at a 'public footpath' signpost to take a well-used track along the raised bank of the beck, passing behind a large caravan site.

Cross the beck on a footbridge and continue alongside the water to Little Braithwaite. Follow the signposted route through the farm and join a surfaced lane. Turn left to descend to the bridge over Newlands Beck, then turn left again towards Ullock at the road junction. The view to the right is along the Vale of Newlands.

Twenty metres after passing the large farmstead of Ullock turn left at a gate with 'public footpath' sign to follow a well-used track along the field boundary to Portinscale. At a surfaced road turn left for 20m, then right, along a path, to continue to the main village street. Turn right to descend to the road junction, then turn left to return to the parking area.

20. Keswick and Latrigg

Length: 4¾ miles.

Summary: The fine viewpoint of Latrigg combines well with the nearby Keswick
                    town to make a circuit, with first rate footpaths and just a little public
                    road. Although not long, this walk is quite demanding in ascent, the
                    summit of Latrigg at 367m (1203ft) being approximately 280m (919ft)
                    above the town centre.

Car Parking: Free car park at the top of Gale Road, used for the popular route to
                    Skiddaw. Take the A591 towards Carlisle from the large roundabout on
                    the Keswick by-pass. Turn right at once towards Ormathwaite. In less
                    than one mile turn sharp right again, by the Underscar Hotel, and
                    proceed to the top of the road. Grid reference 281254.

Map: Ordnance Survey Outdoor Leisure no. 4, The English Lakes, north-
                    western area, 1:25,000 or Landranger no 90, Penrith and Keswick,
                    1:50,000.

Tea Shop

Tucked away in Packhorse Court, the Oasis Café is not easily spot-
ted. However, it is readily accessed from two main streets in
Keswick. The café and bistro is owned and ran by Karin and Anne
who are sisters. Very pleasant waitress service; special requests
such as a second plate when sharing a large toasted teacake, so good
we ordered another one anyway, and an extra teabag to provide
strong tea, were willingly provided. On a winter afternoon the hot
muffins and the toasted teacakes were especially welcome. Good
range of teas, and even more choice of coffees, or mugs of hot chocolate, and selection of cold drinks are all available. Hot dishes are
chalked-up on a blackboard each day. There are also salads such as
Cajun chicken, prawn and apple, cheese with fresh fruit, or probably any variation of ingredients; all served with freshly baked bread.
In high season, when open until mid-evening, the menu has bistro-
type food to provide substantial main meals.

Open: 10.30am to 4.30pm all the year but closed every Tuesday out
of main season. In high-season open until 8pm. Tel: 017687 74974

About the Area

For a brief description of Keswick, see walk no. 21. The splendid little Keswick Museum and Art Gallery is on the line of this walk. Opening is from Easter to the end of October.

Latrigg is held in special affection in the Keswick area as the local, very accessible, hill. Close to the town, its slopes rise steeply to the open top, a fine place for unhindered rambling over easy grass, with the enjoyment of the wonderful views to the south and west.

This route uses a small length of the much lamented former Cockermouth, Keswick and Penrith railway line, opened in 1864 and finally closed in 1972. Much of the trackbed around Keswick has been designated as walkway and cycleway.

The River Greta flows in a beautiful gorge at the base of Latrigg, separating the fell from the town. Much less attractive separation is evident in the obtrusive A66 major road by-pass, cutting its broad swathe across the foot of the hill.

Suspension bridge at Portinscale with Latrigg in the distance

The Walk

Set off by turning left through a kissing gate signposted 'public bridle way, Keswick', along a well-worn downhill track, soon by the top edge of a coniferous plantation. In about 400m fork left by a little 'footpath' sign to climb the side of the hill at a modest gradient.

As height is gained the views steadily improve, eventually to include Derwentwater, the north western group of fells – most obviously Cat Bells, Causey Pike, Hopegill Head, Grisedale Pike and Barf, Bassenthwaite Lake and Skiddaw. At the foot of the north western fells are the villages of Portinscale, Braithwaite and Thornthwaite, whilst Applethwaite sits below Skiddaw. See whether you can pick out the white painted rock known as the 'Bishop of Barf' not far from Thornthwaite.

The path zig zags and is entirely easy to follow on its steady rise to the summit. A seat near the top must be one of the best placed in the whole of the Lake District. Continue along the top to an old wall with gate/stile. Don't go over, but turn right, downhill, to a plantation of youngish conifers. Go over a stile and descend through the plantation on a narrow but adequate path.

At a white arrowed junction turn left for 'Keswick' to zig zag down a steep hillside, aided by steps in places. At a cross-paths go straight on, signposted 'Keswick', to continue the descent. Go over a stile and then down to the road bridge over the by-pass road. Cross the bridge and stay with the surfaced road, gently downhill. In about 400m turn left into the gravelled drive of a large house, Brundholme, 'footpath to Keswick by permission of landowner'. Turn right in 40m and pass along the edge of the house gardens, rich in rhododendrons. Cross high over a little stream, which tumbles joyously down the hillside in its enthusiasm to join the River Greta below.

Go over the top of a sunken lane, pass above the Keswick Bridge timeshare complex and join the public road. Turn left under the old railway bridge, pass the end of the Keswick Hotel and continue to the junction with Station Road. For those with an interest in memorabilia, there are traditional 'AA' signs high on the dormers of the hotel.

A corner may be cut by using a little gate on the left to enter part of the public park, emerging through impressive iron gates, opposite the museum. In either case turn left to cross the River Greta and walk into Keswick town centre along Station Street. The recommended tea shop is to the right, in the access way to Packhorse Court.

Return along Station Road, pass the museum and, in 40m, turn

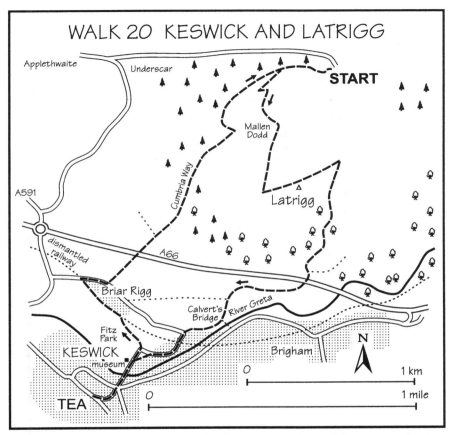

WALK 20 KESWICK AND LATRIGG

Applethwaite
Underscar
START
Mallen Dodd
Cumbria Way
A591
Latrigg
dismantled railway
A66
Briar Rigg
Calvert's Bridge
River Greta
Fitz Park
KESWICK
museum
Brigham
TEA
N
0   1 km
0   1 mile

left to descend to a broad track along one edge of the park playing fields. In less than 200m fork right on a path heading for modern housing. Ignore the obvious kissing gate; bear left and go through another kissing gate 50m or so further.

Ascend to the old railway embankment. Turn left to walk along the embankment; Latrigg is visible over the rooftops. At the end of the embankment, go down to the right and turn right along a residential roadway, Briar Rigg. Turn left in just over 100m into Spooney Green Lane, a 'public bridleway, Skiddaw'. The lane crosses over the by-pass and passes an old farm before the ascent starts in earnest

The excellent rising track is part of the Cumbria Way. Ignore paths to right or left and plod straight on as the track, with good views over the Bassenthwaite area, leads unerringly back to the car park.

21. Keswick and Friar's Crag

Length: 6 miles.

Summary: A fine and varied walk combining a steep ascent to 379m. (1244feet),
                   with a visit to Keswick and a return along the beautiful Derwentwater
                   shore. Underfoot, the paths are generally excellent and easy to follow.
                   Erosion damage on the ascent has been well repaired. Much of the
                   route is in woodland. Friar's Crag, the Ruskin Memorial Stone and the
                   new National Trust Centenary Stone are all found along the way.

Car Parking: National Trust pay and display car park at Great Wood, readily
                   accessed from the Keswick to Borrowdale road, a little more than one
                   and a half miles south of Keswick. Grid reference 271213.

Map: Ordnance Survey Outdoor Leisure no. 4, The English Lakes, north-
                   western area, 1:25,000 or Landranger no. 90, Penrith and Keswick,
                   1:50,000.

Tea Shop

Abrahams, at George Fisher's, is in the roof space of a tall building so
it is quite an ascent through the shop. One almost expects to meet a
famous mountaineer round every corner! The café is on a balcony
overlooking the sales area, and from the roof windows are views of
the hills; displayed is a diagram naming the visible fells. Friendly
waitress service – good choice of savouries including filled rolls, Hill
Shepherd's lunch consisting cheese, pickle, roll and butter, and an
apple. Each day hot specials are listed on the blackboard. There is a
good selection of cakes; apple pie is served with cream or with Cheddar cheese. For tea, there are cakes, muffins, crumpets, and excellent scones. The menu is health conscious too – the establishment
has a Heartbeat Award. Coffee, including espresso, cappuccino, decaffeinated, is available by the cup or in half pint mugs. Various teas,
Horlicks, hot chocolate, even gluhwein! are all available.

On the back of the menu is an intriguing write-up about local
place names – interesting to read whilst waiting for food to arrive. In-
cidentally, in the shop one can hire mountain equipment, including
boots, baby-carriers and many other items – so it really is fascinating
to visit George Fisher's Mountain Emporium.

Open: 10am to 5.30pm (5pm in winter months) Monday – Saturdays
10.30am to 4pm on Sundays. Closed Christmas Day, Boxing Day,
and Easter Sunday. Tel: 017687 72178

About the Area

Close to the east shore of Derwentwater, Walla Crag rises precipitously, with imposing precipices of naked rock, belying its modest height of 379m (1244 feet). Between the crag and the lake the slopes are attractively wooded, for some distance the trees reaching right to the water's edge. This is Great Wood, one of the largest areas of forestry in the district in National Trust ownership.

Also included in the circuit are **Castlehead and Cockshott Woods**, again owned by the National Trust, both well-diversified and particularly good in autumn.

Derwentwater is arguably the most beautiful of all the lakes, enhanced by the four islands, three of which are close to the shoreline and the route of this walk. Views are a particular feature of the walk, ranging from viewpoints at lake shore level, including the celebrated Friar's Crag, to higher levels such as Walla Crag and Castle-

Derwentwater

head. Skiddaw, Blencathra, the Cat Bells ridge and much of Borrowdale are all included

Keswick (*Kase Wick* = cheese town) is a great little town, situated between Skiddaw and the lake. The present town centre, largely Victorian, clusters around the tight little Market Place, with Moot Hall and Tourist Information. Much older is the original parish church of St Kentigern at Great Crosthwaite, now on the fringe of the town. On a religious site claimed to date from AD533 the present fine building is mainly of the 15th century, but with some remaining Norman work. The churchyard entrance gate has the symbols of its founder, St Kentigern – tree, fish, bird and bell – displayed. Inside is a striking white marble memorial to poet laureate Robert Southey, with an epitaph written by his great friend William Wordsworth. Also buried here is Canon Rawnsley, one of the three founders of the National Trust and a great Lakeland environmentalist of his time.

In medieval times Keswick became a great wool centre, with a market charter of the 13th century. Industry arrived in the late 16th century, when German miners opened up the Goldscope Mine in the nearby Newlands valley and other mines were soon developed in the area. Attempts to find marketable quantities of gold failed, but copper, lead and other minerals were mined intermittently until the present century. There was a smelter by the River Greta, to the east of the town. Perhaps best known is the discovery of graphite at Seathwaite in Borrowdale, giving Keswick the distinction of having the world's first pencil industry.

Following the 'discovery' of the Lake District' by eminent early travellers of the 18th century Romantic era, Keswick became highly regarded as a focus for early tourism, later followed by mass tourism after the opening in 1865 of the railway line which connected with the main London, Carlisle and Glasgow line at Penrith. Since then, little has changed apart from the sad closure of the railway line in 1972 and the replacement of the train by the motor car as the means of access. Keswick remains a very popular place indeed, with attractions such as the Cumberland Pencil Museum, Cars of the Stars, Keswick Museum and Art Gallery and lake boating.

Of the four Derwentwater islands, only Derwent Isle is now inhabited, although in the long distant past St Herbert's Island had a hermit's cell. Derwent Isle was the home of the original German miners, later being purchased by a wealthy eccentric named Pocklington who constructed all kinds of folly buildings and staged large scale mock naval battles on the lake around the island.

The Walk

Leave the car park at a gate/stile facing the towering height of Walla Crag to take a path which rises at once. Bear right at a junction in less than 100m then go straight on for 'Ashness Bridge', rising steadily on a well-used stony path.

The next fork is just before Cat Gill. Keep left here to rise to a small gate above the rushing rapids, perhaps best seen from a bridge below, just off the route of the walk. The path soon climbs more steeply, never far above the gill, through light woodland at the southern edge of Great Wood. Close to the head of the gill the valley narrows and deepens to become a steep-sided ravine, with the path bending to the left, still climbing, now close to a wall on the left.

For some distance the path stays close to this wall, a sure guide in mist. There are several stiles and a gate bringing other tracks from the left through the wall. Ignore all these unless wanting short detours to high level viewpoints. Keep left at a junction, continuing to rise on a grassy path, partially through bracken, soon reaching the flat and rather indeterminate top of the hill.

Continue in the same direction along the obvious path, keeping reasonably close to the wall where there are apparent choices of route and going a little to the right at an erosion control area. Go over a stile by a gate and continue the descent to a footbridge over Brockle Beck. Cross and turn left to pass Rakefoot, continuing along the minor roadway for 200m. Turn left at a gate with 'Keswick and Great Wood footpath' signpost and descend to another footbridge over Brockle Beck, then bear right towards Keswick.

Go straight on at the next signpost, soon reaching Springs Wood. At a junction in the wood turn left, avoiding the enticing footbridge ahead. After Springs Farm follow a surfaced residential road. Turn right at a waymarked footpath opposite a house called 'Wood Close' and head for Castlehead Wood.

Rise through the woodland, keeping to the right of the summit of the hill and taking care not to be deflected at apparent forks. The correct route passes a seat. A detour to the summit, a celebrated viewpoint, is short and without difficulty. Descend to the Borrowdale road, go straight across to the roadside footpath, and turn left. In 60m, turn right at a footpath signposted 'To the Lake'.

On reaching Cockshott Wood turn sharp right; soon reaching the large car park situated between Keswick and the lake. Turn right to walk past the pitch and putt course into the town. Use the pedestrian underpass to reach Lake Road. George Fisher's long established emporium of mountain and outdoor equipment is just beyond the National Park Information Centre.

Return past the car park, two sets of public conveniences and the boat landings to head along the broad track leading to Friar's Crag. Along the way are a memorial tablet to Canon Rawnsley and a standing stone memorial to John Ruskin, part concealed among the trees.

After admiring the wonderful view of Borrowdale and the Catbells and Maiden Moor ridge from the Crag, a favourite of Ruskin, back track for a few metres then turn right along a narrow path, descending to join a major track. Turn right to walk along the shore of Strandshag Bay, close to Lord's Island. The path enters a wood at a gate and continues predominantly around the edge of the trees.

Leave the wood at a gate and turn right along an unsurfaced roadway as far as Calf Close Bay, with Rampsholme Island now in view. On the shingle at the edge of the water is the 1996 National Trust Centenary stone, marking 100 years of the Trust in the Lake District.

As the path approaches the road, look out for a National Trust stone pillar, with coin box. Turn left here to a gap in the roadside wall, cross the road to a similar gap, and take the broad track rising back to the car park.

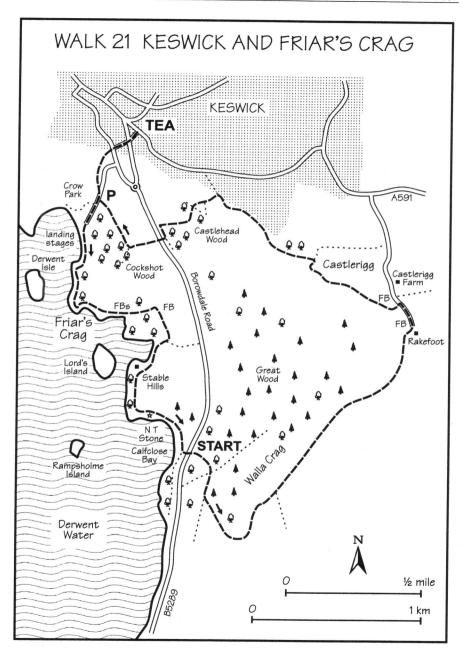

WALK 21 KESWICK AND FRIAR'S CRAG

KESWICK

TEA

Crow Park

P

A591

landing stages

Castlehead Wood

Castlerigg

Castlerigg Farm

Derwent Isle

Cockshot Wood

Borrowdale Road

FB

FBs

FB

FB

Friar's Crag

Rakefoot

Lord's Island

Great Wood

Stable Hills

N T Stone

START

Calfclose Bay

Walla Crag

Rampsholme Island

Derwent Water

N

B5289

O   ½ mile

O   1 km

22. Grange in Borrowdale and Derwentwater

Length: 6¼ miles

Summary: A delightful walk using one of Lakeland's best terrace footpaths to visit Grange in Borrowdale, with the return through the woodlands along the west shore of Derwentwater. No significant ascent and good footpaths throughout. A little more than half a mile along a quiet road.

Car Parking: Small free car park just off the Portinscale to Grange road by the north end of Cat Bells. Grid reference 247212. Some overflow parking spaces by the adjacent roadside.

Map: Ordnance Survey Outdoor Leisure no. 4, The English Lakes, north-western area, 1:25,000 or Landranger no. 90, Penrith and Keswick, 1:50,000.

Tea Shop

Walkers Welcome! so says the sign at Grange Bridge Tea Shop. Outside at the rear is a super terrace overlooking the River Derwent and the fells – an idyllic situation. The time of day will always influence one's choice of refreshment. The "Fellman's lunch" is appealing; this comprises red and white Cheddar cheese with pickle, salad, and granary bread. Local trout from Seathwaite, a few miles further up the Borrowdale Valley is served with salad and baked potato. For lighter fare try the sandwiches, cakes, and scones. Abundant choice of drinks, including milk shakes.

Open: 10am to 7.30pm every day (may close earlier in the winter months). Open all the year. It may be advisable to check availability if visiting out of season. Tel: 017687 77201

About the Area

The situation of Derwentwater, at the point where the wonderful valley of Borrowdale broadens into the Vale of Keswick below the shapely peak of Cat Bells, gives it great scenic advantage. The lake itself, serene, woodland fringed and dotted with islands, is entirely

Grange in Borrowdale

sublime, justifiably regarded by many as Lakeland's finest. What greater accolade could there be?

This walk takes full advantage of this natural generosity. The terraced section along the flank of Cat Bells is rivalled for views and easy walking only by Loughrigg Terrace at Grasmere, whilst the return through Manesty Park and Brandlehow Park is as fine as any lakeside walk in the district.

Much of the western shore of Derwentwater was bought during 1781-5 by Lord William Gordon, brother of the Gordon of the anti-Catholic 'Gordon' riots of 1780. Gordon built a large house to replace a farm at Derwent Bay, and then another at Silver Hill. He re-routed the existing road higher up the hillside and planted large numbers of trees, including oak and several coniferous species, threaded with driveways and footpaths. Gordon's objective was to 'enhance' what he saw as the inherent but not entirely adequate natural beauty of the hillside above the lake, much as the more aware of today's gardeners will incorporate attractive natural features in their overall design. The main difference was that Gordon's 'garden' was the best part of three miles in length!

Fortunately Gordon showed more sensitivity than some of his contemporary improvers of the landscape and, in any case, the ensuing 200 years or so has so mellowed his plantings that few will now complain of artificiality.

Despite its compact size, Grange in Borrowdale is one of the valley's more important settlements, situated by the side of the River Derwent, a little way above the lake and the low-lying, swampy, area at its head. As indicated by the name, the village was originally an outlying 'grange' or grain store in Monastic times, when the ownership of Borrowdale was shared between the powerful abbeys of Furness near Barrow and Fountains in Yorkshire. Because of the width of the river at this point, the approach to Grange is over a long double bridge, both unusual and attractive. The little church of Holy Trinity is mid 19th century.

The Keswick launch on Derwentwater operates a timetabled service from the Keswick boat landings; alternately clockwise and anti-clockwise round the lake, calling at six other jetties. Those at High Brandlehow and Hawse End can be used to incorporate a short (clockwise) or possibly a long (anti-clockwise) boat trip into the walk. From mid March to the end of November departures from Keswick are basically half hourly, with extra sailings quarter-hourly during school summer holidays if there is sufficient demand. A 'walkers' special' leaving Keswick at 0945, direct to Hawse End, can avoid the use of a car for those wishing to start this walk. In winter, departures are hourly, at weekends only, but possibly Monday to Friday on demand. During the Christmas/New Year week there are daily sailings. Tel. 017687 72263 for details and times.

The Walk

Walk back to the public road and turn right, towards Grange, for a short distance. Ignore a track which rises quite steeply towards the summit of Cat Bells, but take the next right turn, an inviting broad track with a 'pubic bridleway' sign. This delectable path keeps to the lower flanks of Cat Bells, a terrace with wonderful views of Derwentwater and across to Walla Crag and Kings How. Behind are

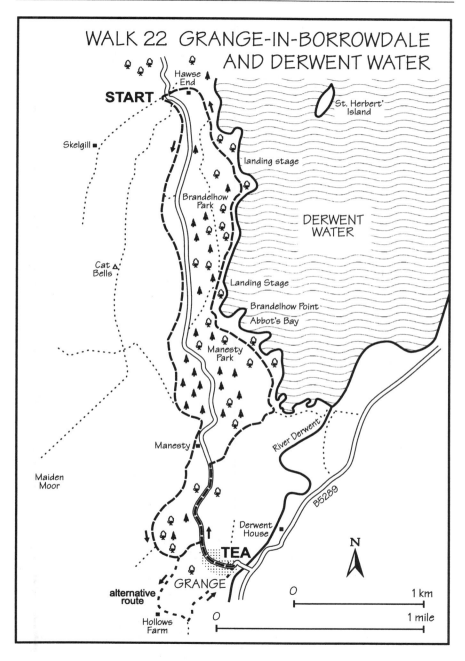

WALK 22 GRANGE-IN-BORROWDALE AND DERWENT WATER

START

Hawse End

Skelgill

St. Herbert' Island

landing stage

Brandelhow Park

DERWENT WATER

Cat Bells

Landing Stage

Brandelhow Point

Abbot's Bay

Manesty Park

Manesty

River Derwent

Maiden Moor

B5289

Derwent House

TEA

N

GRANGE

alternative route

Hollows Farm

0 — 1 km

0 — 1 mile

Skiddaw and Blencathra; ahead are Castle Crag in the Jaws of Bor-rowdale, with the high central mountains beyond.

For some distance no route finding is necessary. At a former quarry the road is rejoined for a few metres only, before the track rises again above Manesty Park. At a fork keep left beside a wall, the upper boundary of woodland. Just beyond the woodland turn left, downhill. At a gate/stile near the bottom, turn right along a narrow path signposted 'permissive path, Hollows Farm, Seatoller'

This path passes above Manesty by the side of the boundary fence. Beyond Manesty the path joins a public right of way. Hereabouts the path is somewhat diffuse as it passes above High Close. Stay fairly close to the fence on the left, soon crossing a bustling stream. At the end of the wood turn left by a small sewage works, downhill towards Grange village, passing a yellow arrow waymark on a post.

To go direct to Grange, go through a farm gate on the left and take a narrow path across a field, descending to the left to join the public road. Turn right into the village; the chosen tea shop is at the far end, by the river.

For the slightly longer route, don't go through the farm gate, but bear right to stay with the major track to Hollows Farm. After passing the farm, turn left along the broad track leading directly into Grange.

On leaving the tea shop, walk back through the village and con-tinue along the public road for approximately half a mile, passing the Borrowdale Gates Hotel. Immediately after crossing Ellers Beck turn right at a gate with a 'Lodore' signpost. Go along the well-used path, then through a kissing gate by the corner of a wall. After a sec-ond kissing gate fork left by some gorse bushes.

The lake soon comes into view as the path forks again. Either fork will do here; the paths come together again a little further on. That to the right is on the right of way shown by Ordnance Survey. Turn left at a junction and pass over sections of wooden causeway over swampy ground. The lakeside path is through attractive woodland.

On reaching a house named 'The Warren', behind Abbot's Bay, turn right along an access roadway, passing through a gate. Brandle-how Bay is a little further. Keep left at a junction, pass 'Brandlehow', where there is a little signpost, and leave the bay along a broad, stony, track rising to the left.

Turn right through a small gate into woodland and keep to the lower path, to High Brandlehow jetty, where the launch may be taken back to Hawse End. The route now stays close to the lake shore to reach Low Brandlehow jetty, another opportunity to take the boat.

On reaching a division of the ways, turn left along a track just outside the wood, soon rising towards a large house, Hawse End. Join a major track after a kissing gate and turn right to follow 'Lingholm, Keswick'. After passing below the large house, join a surfaced roadway and keep right. At a coach turning area turn left, uphill, along a 'Cat Bells' signposted footpath. Join the public road in a short distance and go left, uphill, to the cul de sac road and the car park.

If using the launch, from the boat landing at Hawse End walk up the path to the Hawse End access drive and cross to the 'Cat Bells' footpath mentioned above.

23. Seatoller, Rosthwaite and Castle Crag

Length: 4 miles (shorter version – 3 miles)

Summary: A fine circuit which has, in miniature, most of the essential features of a Lake District walk – a sharp little peak, some steep ascents and descents on stony paths, woodland, a gentle ramble by the side of a lovely river and two attractive settlements. Apart from a rather awkward section after passing the youth hostel, the paths are without difficulty.

Car Parking: National Trust car park with public conveniences at Seatoller. Grid reference 245138.

Map: Ordnance Survey Outdoor Leisure no. 4, The English Lakes, north-western area, 1:25,000 or Landranger no. 90, Penrith and Keswick.

Tea Shop

"Flock In" is a tea room right on the walkers' track – a particularly welcome sight after a walk on the fells or even following a short stroll to justify indulgence. For thirsty walkers tea and coffee are served in half pint or pint measures – or why not try good old fashioned Vimto! Savouries include cheese on toast and bacon baps. Specialities home-made at Yew Tree Farm include authentic Borrowdale tea bread- delicious! Or try the unique "Flock In gorgeous" – a kind of chocolate shortbread with nuts and raisins. The café is owned and operated by the family at Yew Tree Farm (just across the lane) and accommodation is available at the farm.

Open: 10am to 5pm (sometimes later) every day but weekends only in November. Closed December and January. Hours could just possibly be unreliable so worth checking first if relying on this facility. Tel: 017687 77675

About the Area

For many, Borrowdale is the finest of Lakeland's numerous valleys. Its considerable length and rich variety of landscape, including the traditional buildings of the small villages and hamlets, and its penetration to the heart of the great central mountains make an unbeatable combination. In particular, the wide area of green fields above

Seatoller

the famous 'Jaws of Borrowdale', generous by Lakeland agricultural standards, is cut off by the constriction and it is easy to appreciate its former isolation, the consequent insularity of its people, and the 'Kings of Borrowdale' title applied to their leaders centuries ago. Centre of this delectable area is Rosthwaite, with two inns, shop and the selected tea shop supplementing its basic farming activity. Seatoller is another attractive settlement, with tourist information, a little further up the valley, at the point where the road makes its escape by the steep and high climb to the Honister Pass and on to Buttermere.

Castle Crag is a remarkable little peak, at about 300m (985ft), the only summit of less than 1,000ft to appear in the late A. Wainwright's classic mountain guides. What a distinction, earned, no doubt by the sharpness of the peak and the uncompromising steepness on all sides, as the Crag stands well clear of the bulky fell of which it is really an off-shoot. The woodland on the slopes adds to the attraction and hides most of the extensive quarrying, which left many scars and holes. The side of the Crag overlooking the river has caves which, earlier this century, were inhabited in summer by a well known eccentric, Millican Dalton.

The Walk

Walk to the road and turn right to pass through the tiny village of Seatoller. As is obvious from the gradient, this is the start of the Honister Pass. Hause Gill tumbles noisily to the left. As the road bends to the left, turn right to climb the roadside bank, up to a gate.

Go up the steep hillside on a well-marked path, engineered in part, through the bracken. To the left is Seatoller Fell, below Grey Knotts; behind is the great bulk of Glaramara. Keep left at a fork and rise to join a broad, stony, track. Turn left for a short distance, facing up towards the Honister Pass.

At a cairn with a discreet little signpost fork right towards 'Grange'. Rise over grass to a gate in a wall and turn right along a path on the far side of the wall. The ascent soon comes to an end. This well-used path is part of the designated 'Allerdale Ramble'. The path passes behind the minor hill, High Doat. Ahead, Castle Crag and King's How are soon in view.

Cross a gill on a footbridge and enjoy the view of the former 'kingdom' of upper Borrowdale below. Rosthwaite is soon visible. Cross another bridge and continue to the junction where the path from Dale Head via Rigghead Quarries joins on the left.

Turn right here and descend to New Bridge for the shorter version of the walk, omitting Castle Crag.

The full walk continues by crossing Tongue Gill on two footbridges, followed by a stony section of path. Across Borrowdale the Langstrath Valley joins the main valley below Stonethwaite hamlet. Behind Stonethwaite is the abrupt and soaring Eagle Crag. As the path starts its descent, the views of Derwentwater and Skiddaw to the north are a sample of what can be seen from the summit of Castle Crag.

In a short distance, downhill, look for a right turn and a path leading up to a stile over a wall. The precipices of the Crag look formidable but fear not, there is a perfectly safe way to the top. On the right is a seat with a plaque to Sit William Hamer, who gave this land to the nation in 1939.

Go over a ladder stile and an ordinary stile and continue along the obvious path, soon reaching a junction. For the top go left and tackle the enormous quarry spoil heap, then bear left above the rim of the summit quarry. The views include Skiddaw and Blencathra to the north, Helvellyn to the east, and an array of fells to the south, includ-

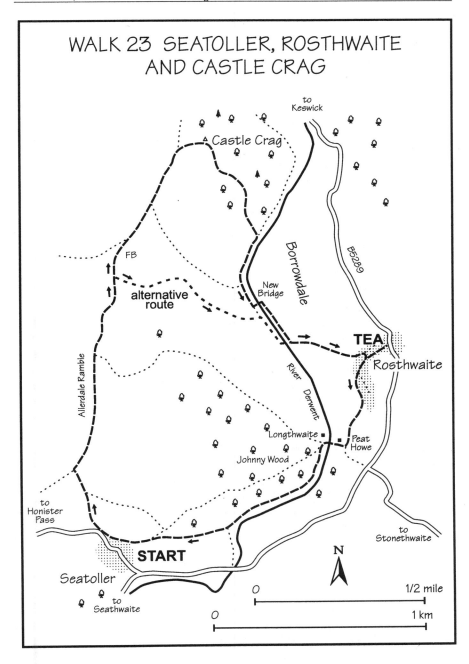

WALK 23 SEATOLLER, ROSTHWAITE AND CASTLE CRAG

to Keswick

Castle Crag

Borrowdale

B5289

FB

New Bridge

alternative route

TEA

Rosthwaite

Allerdale Ramble

River Derwent

Longthwaite

Peat Howe

Johnny Wood

to Honister Pass

to Stonethwaite

START

Seatoller

to Seathwaite

N

0   1/2 mile

0   1 km

ing Scafell Pike, Scafell and Great Gable. Descend back to the junction and turn left to a ladder stile.

To omit the summit, turn right at the junction to go direct to the ladder stile. After the stile the path descends quite steeply, over grass initially, to a gate in a wall. Enter woodland to continue the steep descent to the valley bottom path, joined at a gate/stile. Turn right to follow this broad, easy, route to Rosthwaite, crossing the River Derwent at New Bridge or, for the more adventurous, by the stepping stones 300m or so upstream.

The teashop is on the left, opposite Yew Tree Farm. Note the weather vane on the roof. Leave the teashop and take the surfaced roadway to the left of Yew Tree Farm, passing some fine traditional cottages. In approximately 100m turn right to leave the lane immediately before the house named 'Stone Croft'. In 20m turn left through a gate, signposted 'Path to Longthwaite Y.H.A.'. Go along the edge of the field to a waymarked stile and then diagonally right to a gate with a huge boulder built into the adjacent wall. Bear left to Peat Howe hamlet. Note the slate on edge boundary to the left, rare except in the Hawkshead area.

Turn right along the surfaced roadway, cross the bridge over the river, and bear left to pass across the front of the youth hostel. After a kissing gate there is a short scrambly section by the side of the river, with a fixed chain to give assurance in the most awkward part. Take reasonable care and there is no real danger. At this point the river is progressively cutting away the end of a long glacial moraine, revealing the composition of the debris piled up by the moving ice a few thousand years ago.

The path continues by a wall along the lower edge of Johnny Wood, maintained, like so much of Borrowdale, by the National Trust. As a large holiday centre building is approached, go right, up to a gate in a wall then bear left. Seatoller is soon in view, the path going through a gate/stile direct into the car park.

24. Rosthwaite and Watendlath

Length:	5 miles
Summary:	Allow a good half day for this walk over the high ground, which separates Watendlath from Borrowdale. Although the highest point of the walk does not exceed 420m (1378ft), there is a long, steep, climb up the side of the valley opposite Stonethwaite and a lesser climb after Watendlath. Along the high ground, after Dock Tarn, the path winds over a mixture of rough rock and boggy ground before descending to Watendlath hamlet, beautifully placed on the edge of its tarn.
Car Parking:	National Trust pay and display car park in Rosthwaite village, by the public conveniences. Grid reference 257148.
Map:	Ordnance Survey Outdoor Leisure no.4, The English Lakes, north-western area, 1:25,000 or Landranger no. 90, Penrith and Keswick, 1:50,000.

Tea Shop

Watendlath is a unique and remote hamlet and we were pleased to find a refreshment facility here. Caffle House is certainly not a "pretty pretty" tea shop but a robust café for walkers. Seating is mainly outdoors. Sandwiches, scones, cakes, and ice cream are available, as are tea, coffee, and cold drinks.

Open: from two weeks before Easter to end of October 10.30am to 5pm (sometimes earlier or later!) every day. Tel: 017687 77219

About the Area

With two inns and a post office/general store, Rosthwaite is the focal point of the upper part of Borrowdale. Despite its popularity with visitors, it is still very much an unspoilt farming village.

Watendlath is the only settlement in the charming shallow valley formed by the Watendlath Beck, where several farms once competed for the small amount of usable land. The hamlet is at the end of a narrow cul de sac road, which leaves the road in Borrowdale below the much photographed Ashness Bridge, of chocolate box fame (or notoriety!)

The comparatively little known **Dock Tarn** is set in a shallow depression among the confused landscape of broken rocky ground which is so typical of the Borrowdale area. Although not competing with, say, Stickle Tarn in Langdale for dramatic setting, it does have a quiet charm. The line of the right of way shown here by the Ordnance Survey is curious. Whilst accepting that hill walkers have many admirable attributes and may well lead exemplary lives, I have yet to encounter any with the ability to walk on water which is clearly a requisite of following the Ordnance Survey line. I have to confess that, being a little uncertain of my own righteousness and not wanting boots full of water, I didn't dare put it to the test; other ordinary mortals are advised to follow the alternative line set out below.

The Walk

Walk back to the main road in Rosthwaite; turn left for 30m and then turn right at a signpost 'public bridleway Stonethwaite and Watendlath'. Cross the bridge over Stonethwaite Beck. The house ahead is Hazel Bank, on the site of the fictional 'Herries' which was the home of the hero of Walpole's Herries series of novels.

Turn right immediately after the bridge; there are two signposts, both mentioning Stonethwaite. The excellent level path leaves the main valley, bending gently to the left along the tributary valley of Stonethwaite Beck, in its higher reaches known as Langstrath. Keep straight on at a junction close to Stonethwaite hamlet, following a 'Grasmere, Greenup Edge' signpost. Ahead the great rocky mound of Eagle Crag guards the junction of Greenup Gill with the main valley.

Immediately after a gate turn left, uphill, at an old 'Dock Tarn' signpost. Initially over grass, the track becomes stony as it passes through oak woodland, rising steeply for a total of about 270m (886ft). Much of this well used path is engineered and the line is never farm from Withy Grass Gill, tumbling and rushing over rapids and little falls on the right.

After a stile over a wall the country becomes more open and the gradient eases. Behind, Honister youth hostel stands out in the distance, perched high above the intervening depression of Borrowdale. There is a stone cairn as Dock Tarn is approached. As suggested above, ignore the Ordnance Survey here and go to the left of the tarn, along a clear path close to the edge of the water. After the tarn the path twists and turns over rock as it avoids the worst of some

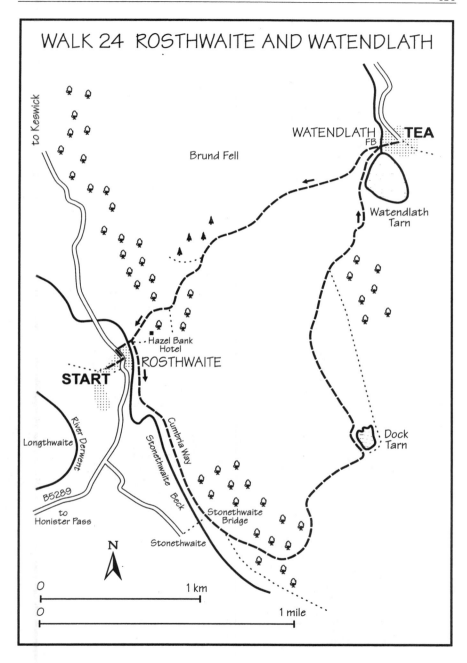

WALK 24 ROSTHWAITE AND WATENDLATH

to Keswick

WATENDLATH
FB
TEA

Brund Fell

Watendlath
Tarn

Hazel Bank
Hotel
ROSTHWAITE

START

Longthwaite

River Derwent

Cumbria Way

Stonethwaite Beck

Dock
Tarn

B5289
to
Honister Pass

Stonethwaite
Bridge

Stonethwaite

N

0   1 km

0   1 mile

boggy ground. It is never really difficult to follow; the general line is always close to north.

In less than half a mile there is a steep descent and Watendlath hamlet and tarn come into view. Distant Skiddaw is seen ahead. Descend to a kissing gate close to a stream and keep right at a 'Watendlath' sign on a post. The path soon becomes a broad, stony, lane leading directly to the hamlet.

Returning from Watendlath keep right at the major fork to climb steadily along the very well used track towards Rosthwaite. Once over the top Borrowdale comes into view. At a junction turn right through a gate, still descending. Rejoin the outward route close to the bridge over Stonethwaite Beck and return to the car park.

Rosthwaite Village shop

25. St John's in the Vale and High Rigg

Length:	5¼ miles
Summary:	This walk starts at Legburthwaite hamlet and climbs over High Rigg, a long and knobbly hill, to reach the church of St John's in the Vale. The return is a gentle walk along a former coffin road on one side of the beautiful valley. The path over the hill winds among the rocky outcrops, a little wet in places, but otherwise never difficult underfoot. It is only partially shown on Ordnance Survey maps.
Car Parking:	Substantial free car park, with toilets, in Legburthwaite. Finding the entrance needs care. Grid reference 318195.
Map:	Ordnance Survey Outdoor Leisure, The English Lakes, either no.4, north-western area or no. 5, north-eastern area, 1:25,000 or Landranger no. 90, Penrith and Keswick, 1:50,000.

Tea Shop

The tea garden at Low Bridge End Farm was discovered and recommended by our publisher. It is an unusual venue, not far from the road in St John's in the Vale but accessed only from the footpath. The property has been in the family of Sarah Chaplin-Brice for several generations. Now Sarah and her husband Graham with their family live and work here and the atmosphere is very friendly; they really are pleased to see walkers. One may have good quality coffee, tea, steaming hot chocolate, Bovril, or cold drinks. Home-made cakes and wrapped chocolate biscuits are available. Very limited range but nothing is too much trouble so always ask! The terrace is the favourite but if the weather is poor there is some seating in the sun lounge.

Open: every day dawn 'til dusk throughout the year except 24th and 25th December. Tel: 01768 779242

About the Area

High Rigg is an area of steep-sided high ground approximately two miles in length, separating the valley of St John's in the Vale from the

Blencathra from St John's in the Vale

less well defined Nadder Valley, which carries the main A591 Ambleside to Keswick road. On the fell there are several tops of not dissimilar height, some with their own names, such as Wren Crag, Mart Crag and Yew Crag, but the summit described by the late A. Wainwright – 354m. (1163ft) – is very much at the north (church) end and is clearly marked by a cairn. Its detached situation makes High Rigg a very good viewpoint for the Helvellyn ridge, Thirlmere, Skiddaw and, most of all, shapely Blencathra (Saddleback).

St John's church was originally one of five chapels of the old church at Crosthwaite, Keswick. The present building dates from 1845 but there is much evidence of an older church or churches on this site, going back at least to 1554. There is a sundial dated 1635. To present day eyes the situation might seem to be rather odd, but the road past the church used to be an important link between the Nadder and St John's valleys and the church conveniently served the farming communities in both valleys. As with so many Lakeland country churches the building blends beautifully into the landscape, almost a part of the natural scene. Among those buried here is John Richardson, a celebrated Cumberland dialect poet who was born nearby in 1817, helped his father to build the present church, and was schoolmaster at the adjacent school for 22 years. He died at Bridge House in 1886.

On the hillside not far away is a simple but touching little memorial stone, vaguely marked on the Ordnance Survey map. It is to 'David Gerald Pennycook. Who loved these fells. Died 13th June, 1964. Aged 10 years'.

The Walk

Leave the car park by the small gate at the far end and turn left along the broad roadway leading to the main road. Turn right to cross St John's Beck on the road bridge. Turn right again at a gate/ladder stile then, in 20m, fork left, uphill, at a waymark, to commence the initial climb. Keep left at another fork and continue to climb steeply.

The path is good throughout and is always clear on the ground. Despite the modest altitude, this is a real Lakeland hill climb, with views which widen as height is gained. Behind, Thirlmere is framed between the isolated hump of Great How and the long side of Bleaberry Fell, High Seat and High Tove, whilst further to the left Helvellyn and the other tops along its ridge outstrip them all in height.

The first minor summit is Wren Crag. From here, Blencathra is supreme, dominating the northerly view over the Vale of St John. The path continues to be very obvious, rising and falling among the rocky outcrops. At a post with a waymark and 'footpath' sign keep left as directed, passing close below Mart Crag and Yew Crag.

Descend a little to a ladder stile, then climb steadily beside a wall. As progress is made, the views now include Skiddaw and Clough Head, the impressive northern end of the Helvellyn range. Keep left at an apparent fork and head for the cairn-crowned High Rigg summit, (which is not quite where it appears to be on the Ordnance Survey maps) a diversion of 25m from the line of the footpath. The views are surprisingly extensive.

Start the descent by rejoining the main path, soon reaching a fork. Take the left of the two broad, grassy, tracks through the bracken and then descend steeply on grass towards the buildings by the church. To see the memorial stone turn left before the kissing gate at the bottom to follow a well used track through the bracken. The memorial is about 100m WSW of the angle of the wall, which encloses a tree plantation adjoining the Diocesan Youth Centre. It is 50m beyond a

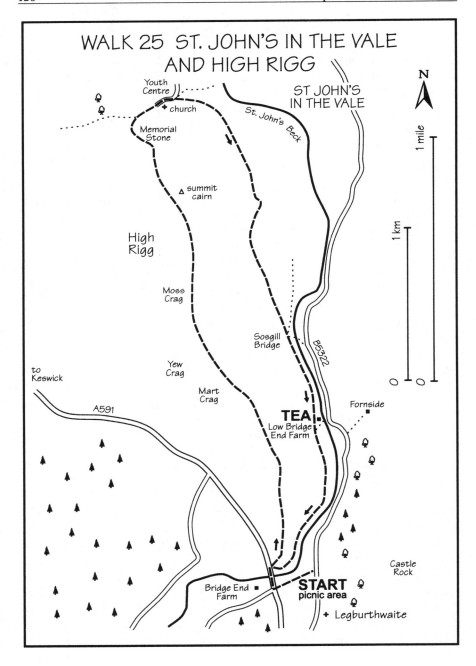

WALK 25 ST. JOHN'S IN THE VALE
AND HIGH RIGG

tiny stream, at the crest of a low cliff. If not visiting the memorial, go through the kissing gate and join the road, turning right.

From the memorial go down to the road and turn right. After a gate/stile the road is surfaced. Follow the road past the church and, in less than 100m, turn right at a gate/stile with 'bridleway' sign to take an excellent broad stony track, gently downhill at first. This is the 'corpse' or 'coffin' road, continuing attractively along the side of the Vale. The ruins of a substantial former farmstead are passed and Sosgill Bridge, a former packhorse bridge, is visible below.

Keep to the right, on a footpath along the valley side, at a junction where the bridleway goes to the left to join the valley bottom path. The way, now narrower and more winding, goes through a small plantation of young trees before reaching Low Bridge End Farm with the tea room and garden.

After refreshment, continue along the same path, passing a rocky area before traversing a steep hillside above St John's Beck. Young children may well need restraint here.

Descend to the gate/ladder stile giving access to the main road and turn left to return to the car park

26. Mungrisdale and Bowscale Tarn

Length: 6¾ miles

Summary: An ascent of Bowscale Fell, not difficult to climb despite its height of
                  702m. (2304ft), one of the remote and comparatively little visited
                  northern group of fells. Included is Bowscale Tarn, set like a jewel in a
                  classic hanging valley. The return route visits the hamlets of
                  Mungrisdale, Bowscale and Mosedale. The majority of the way is on
                  excellent footpaths, with two miles along a quiet road.

Car Parking: Small roadside parking area at the south end of Bowscale. Grid
                  reference 360316. Alternatively, use a small car park by the
                  crossroads in Mosedale. No public conveniences on this walk.

Map: Ordnance Survey Outdoor Leisure no. 5, The English Lakes, north-
                  eastern area, 1:25,000 or Landranger no. 90, Penrith and Keswick,
                  1:50,000.

Tea Shop

Driving along the road towards Caldbeck we came across a sign for a
tea room and it was a super discovery of an unusual venue –
Mosedale Quaker Meeting House. Originally given to the Society of
Friends in 1739, the building was used towards the end of the last
century by travelling preachers, not necessarily Quakers, and then
as a chapel of Mungrisdale Church. In 1971, The Society of Friends
in Carlisle were given permission to restore the building and to use it
not only for religious meetings but also as a museum and to serve a
limited range of refreshments to the public. It is managed, apparently very smoothly, by volunteers on a rota basis. The menu is understandably small but perfectly adequate – home-made cakes are
delivered by local people on a regular basis. Try the buttered tea
bread, biscuits, tea, fruit juices, good quality coffee in individual fil-
ters; if visiting at lunch time try "The Shepherd's Lunch" – cheese,
roll, pickle, and dates. The Meeting House is a marvellously peaceful place to visit.

Open: 11am to 5pm every day from May until September. Tel: not
available

About the Area

Bowscale Fell is a great rounded hump on the eastern edge of the
comparatively remote northern group of fells. There are extensive

Mungrisdale church

views across the broad valley of the River Eden. This fell's great advantage is its tarn, a little jewel set in a classic hanging valley, with the ice-plucked Tarn Crags cradling it closely. Apparently a favourite excursion for Victorian tourists, it is perhaps fortunate that fashions have changed and the tarn is now usually a place of solitude. Please don't prove me wrong by marching up in large parties!

Bounded on the north by the River Caldew and on the south by the River Glenderamackin, which turns south to become the River Greta before joining the River Derwent at Keswick, the fell forms the Derwent/Eden watershed. A curious feature, pointed out by A. Wainright, is that the western slopes drain to the Eden in the east, whilst the eastern slopes drain to the Derwent, in the west.

Mungrisdale, Bowscale and Mosedale are hamlets strung along the little road, which connects the main A66 with Hesket Newmarket and Caldbeck. This road clings to the foot of the scarp of Bowscale and Carrock Fells. All three are no nonsense everyday working settlements, very much in harmony with the landscape. The tiny church of St Kentigern at Mungrisdale dates from the mid 18th century although the present building is by no means the first on this site. The form and the scale seem to be absolutely right for the situation. Inside is a three decker pulpit. Mungrisdale also has an inn.

The Walk

From the informal car parking area at Bowscale walk to the hamlet and immediately fork left at a 'public bridleway, Bowscale Tarn' signpost to take a broad track rising gently up the hillside. From Mosedale walk back along the roadside.

No route finding is necessary on this ascent to the tarn. The lovely track is always easy to follow although it does steepen a little and become narrower after Drycombe Beck is passed. In the valley below most noticeable is the farm complex of Roundhouse, with a circular – or is octagonal? – building which presumably gives the farm its name. Bear left into the combe and sit by the edge of the tarn.

To continue, there is an obvious steep semi-path on grass up through Tarn Crags opposite. This route is steep and awkward and is not recommended. Better is to retrace steps for under 100m and, as the path bends right, to take a just visible minor path on the left which contours across the hillside to go round the end of Tarn Crags. The path becomes more distinct as progress is made.

As this path rises to the top edge of the scarp, leave it to turn sharp left and continue along the top edge of the scarp, heading for the now visible summit. There is no real path here; choose the easiest route over short grass, bending to the right as the summit is approached. This is the steepest part of the walk but there is no difficulty.

The top is crowned with a pile of stones and a crude shelter. The extensive views include the backs of Skiddaw and Blencathra and most of the lesser Northern fells at close quarters and, further, the Buttermere fells, Clough Head, Helvellyn, Fairfield, the High Street group. Across the Eden valley is the long line of the Pennine Hills.

From the top continue the same line, now with a distinct path, for a little more then 300m At a cross paths, marked by a small cairn, turn left along a minor path with a stone marker. This path descends across the flank of the Tongue, the ridge on the left, soon joining a more pronounced path. The excellent path loses height at a reasonable gradient.

Near the bottom, join a wider path at a cairn and carry on down to the River Glenderamackin, reached at the confluence with Bulfell Beck. Cross the latter on a footbridge. Reach a gate at the edge of Mungrisdale hamlet, join the public road, and turn left to return to Bowscale and the tea room at Mosedale. (Non-purists can, of course, reach the tea room by car)

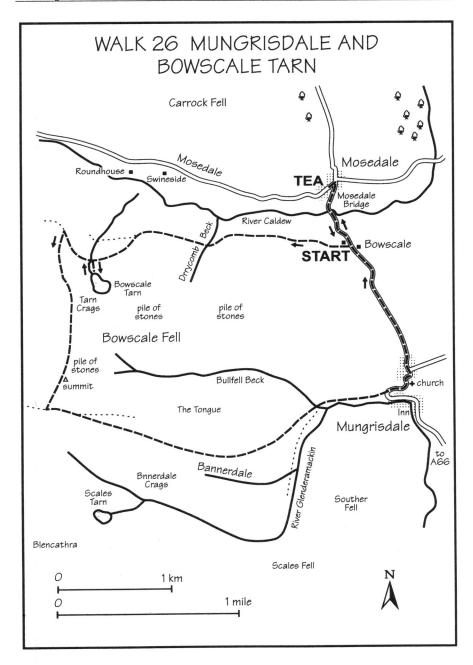

WALK 26 MUNGRISDALE AND BOWSCALE TARN

Carrock Fell

Mosedale

Roundhouse ■

Swineside

Mosedale

TEA

Mosedale Bridge

River Caldew

Drycomb Beck

Bowscale

START

Bowscale Tarn

Tarn Crags

pile of stones

pile of stones

Bowscale Fell

pile of stones

△ summit

Bullfell Beck

church

The Tongue

Inn

Mungrisdale

pile of stones

Bannerdale

Bnnerdale Crags

River Glenderamackin

to A66

Scales Tarn

Souther Fell

Blencathra

Scales Fell

0   1 km

0   1 mile

N

27. Hesket Newmarket

Length: 5½ miles

Summary: A varied tramp across farming country and moorland to visit a disused
mine, with the return along the old mine roadway, surfaced road and
more farmland. Some of the route is across rough grazing land, without
obvious footpath. Almost two miles of the total is beside minor roads. A
high proportion of the numerous stiles on the outward part of the route
can be avoided by using the road alternative suggested below. The
total ascent is about 250m (853ft).

Car Parking: Small free car park at the lower end of Hesket Newmarket, on the right
beyond the Green. Grid reference 342386. No public conveniences in
Hesket Newmarket.

Map: Ordnance Survey Outdoor Leisure no. 7, The English Lakes, north-
eastern area, 1:25,000 or Landranger no. 90, Penrith and Keswick,
1:50,000.

Tea Shop

Liz Crosland started this appealing little café in 1996. It is part of the
post office/store which is owned and ran by Mr & Mrs Crosland. Liz
makes almost everything on the premises including the soup and
bread rolls. Try the John Peel tart – an exotic currant mixture with
ground almonds and candied peel or Rum Nicky made with dried
fruit, apple, and ginger – both are equally delicious especially when
served with cream. Cakes include cherry, date, and chocolate. Very
pleasant to sit outside when the weather is suitable for the shop is at
the heart of village life.

Open: 10am to 5pm minimum each day but closed on Sundays –
open all the year. Tel: 016974 78229

About the Area

Less well provided with facilities than its near neighbour Caldbeck,
Hesket Newmarket is a quieter village, its only street dividing to enclose an elongated green. But, believe it or not, Hesket did have a
market charter for about 100 years from the mid 18th century, when
it must, by definition, have ranked as a town. The market was never

entirely successful although the 'market cross' building and a bull ring do remain as evidence of those grander times.

The **Caldbeck Fells**, rising to the south from the two villages, have long been one of Lakeland's most productive sources of minerals. So long, in fact, that the incoming German miners of Elizabethan times re-opened several workings which were already old. The minerals mined in the area included lead, copper, barytes and tungsten. Production ceased as recently as the 1960s. The turning point of this walk is the site of the former Sandbeds Mine, opened in 1946 and closed a few years later when it was obvious that the yield was continuing to be poor. The machinery was dismantled and the workings were closed.

The village street from the market cross

The Walk

Walk away from the road, across the grass behind the car park, pass a seat and a 'public footpath' sign and go over a gated stile in the wall on the left. Keep close to the fence on the right, go over a stile at the top of the field and bend left as indicated by the yellow arrow waymark. Go to a waymarked farm gate and bear right, diagonally across the next field, to another waymarked stile.

The route is rising gently all the way, to yet another arrowed stile (yes – there are rather a lot on this walk!), a gap in the fence at the top, and a stile on the left in 25m. After more stiles, reach a farm access lane, with Stott Ghyll Farm in a dip on the left.

Go across the lane and take a route to by-pass the farm, keeping well to the right of the little wooded valley. Cross the field to a way-marked stile, then keep close to the fence on the right for about a quarter of a mile to reach a surfaced road.

If stiles and farmland don't appeal, this road leaves Hesket New-market at the top of the village; a left turn just above the tea shop, and is sufficiently quiet to be acceptable to walkers.

Turn left to walk through Wood Hall, a considerable farmstead, noting a dated stone in the wall on the left at the far end. Almost opposite turn right through a farm gate. The signpost here is well hidden behind a wall. Cross a minor stream, pass a farm pond and rise to the left hand of two stiles. Proceed across wilder pastures, rising towards the Caldbeck Fells. There is little to follow on the ground, but the route aims well to the right of the plantation ahead, the compass bearing being about 230 degrees.

The site of the mine is visible before a ladder stile over a wall on the right is reached. The views behind, over the shallow valley containing the village, are dominated by two wind electricity generators, with the Pennine Hills in the distance. Go over, note the 'danger, old mine workings', cross a little stream and follow the now well marked path over grass towards the mine.

Pass large areas desolated by mine spoil, the metallic contamination obviously seriously inhibiting the growth of vegetation. Immediately above this area the roadway which forms the first part of the return route strikes off to the left. To visit the upper part of the old workings carry on beyond the high spoil heaps. In truth, the mine isn't very exiting; presumably for reasons of safety all the various holes have been infilled and fences surround any which could be dangerous.

Return to the roadway and turn right, downhill. This stony track provides excellent walking as it descends towards Calebreck, a lonely farm huddled behind a few trees, which provide shelter from the cold winds of this harsh landscape. Cross Blea Gill, then another

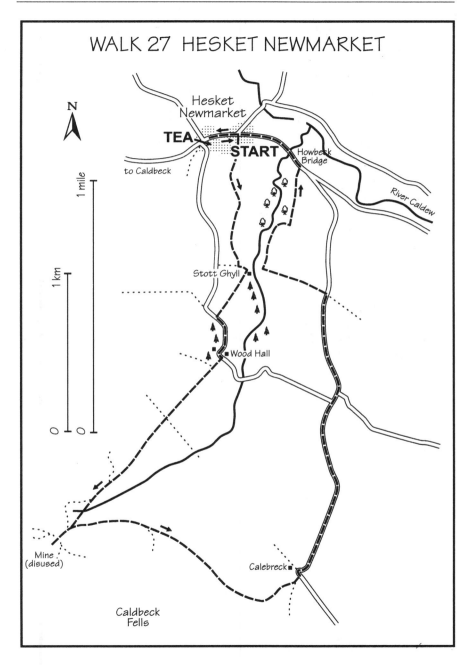

WALK 27 HESKET NEWMARKET

N

Hesket
Newmarket

TEA
START
Howbeck
Bridge

to Caldbeck

River Caldew

1 mile

1 km

Stott Ghyll

Wood Hall

Mine
(disused)

Calebreck

Caldbeck
Fells

small stream and pass a vehicular barrier before joining a minor road by a cattle grid, close to the farm.

Turn left to follow the road, initially uphill, for about 1¼ miles. There are grass verges for those who hate the feel of tarmac and, by a roadside farm, banks of snowdrops in February. Pass Pasture Lane Farm, then roads to left and right. Immediately before a house, The Cottage, dated 1695 with an outbuilding dated 1680; turn left over a waymarked stile to follow a garden-avoiding diversion of the old right of way. To continue along the road provides an equally satisfactory return to Hesket Newmarket.

Descend to cross a tiny stream, go up the bank and turn right to pass behind The Cottage. At the field boundary turn left, follow the fence to a gate/stile and continue the same line across the next field. Stott Ghyll Farm comes into view in its hollow. Turn right immediately before a fence with gate; there is a 'path' sign. Walk along the top of a pretty little wooded valley, keeping right as a fence is reached.

Turn right at a post with yellow arrow, then left at a similar post in 40m to follow a broad track towards a large farm. Go through gates, passing waymarks, to reach the public road. Turn left to return to Hesket Newmarket and the car park. The tea shop, with Post Office/stores, is beyond the car park, at the top end of the village.

28. Caldbeck

Length: 4¼ miles

Summary: A comparatively gentle walk through the delightful Howk gorge and
                     over the sparse farmland between the village and the Caldbeck Fells.
                     A small amount of ascent at generally easy gradients; some mud but
                     otherwise good underfoot on grass and lanes. Two overgrown stiles.

Car Parking: Free public car park in Caldbeck. Grid reference 323399. Public
                     conveniences, probably closed in winter, 200m distant.

Map: Ordnance Survey Outdoor Leisure no. 7, The English Lakes, north-
                     eastern area, 1:25,000 or Landranger no. 90, Penrith and Keswick,
                     1:50,000.

Tea Shop

The chosen venue in Caldbeck is The Old Smithy – a gift shop and
tea room. It is quite small, seating only about sixteen, with a small
additional outdoor area. Friendly service from Tricia Harrison and
her assistants. The menu includes sandwiches, toasties, and jacket

The Forge tea shop

potatoes with a variety of fillings, scones, muffins, crumpets, and teacakes; and to drink, choose tea or coffee by the mug or cup. Fresh orange juice and other cold drinks are also available.

Open: January – March, Saturdays and Sundays only. April and May, every day but closed Tuesdays and Wednesdays. June to September, every day but closed on Wednesdays. October – December, everyday but closed on Tuesdays and Wednesdays. Hours 10am – 6pm in summer and 10am to 5pm in winter. Tel: 016974 78246

About the Area

Caldbeck is a fine village on the northern fringe of the Lake District, just inside the boundary of the National Park. Its remoteness from towns contributes to an air of sturdy independence, with its own church, inn, village store/petrol station, clog maker and tea shop.

The 6th century St Kentigern (or Mungo), Bishop of Glasgow, is said to have preached here and to have carried out baptisms in a well still visible by the side of the bridge over the Cald Beck. The church is appropriately dedicated. The present structure is originally of the 12th century, much modified, but still a building of great interest. Seen inside are stained glass windows depicting St Kentigern and St Cuthbert and a lovely font. In the churchyard the prime attractions are the gravestones of John Peel and Mary Harrison (née Robinson), the celebrated 'Maid of Buttermere'.

From the 13th to the present century, mining for a variety of minerals in the nearby Caldbeck Fells has ebbed and flowed and the water of the Cald Beck and its tributary Gill Beck has powered an array of corn, textile, paper and bobbin mills. In the 19th century, at the height of this industrial activity with its associated wealth, there were no less than six inns and a small brewery in the village. Priest's Mill, last operational in the 1930s, has been converted to use as a craft workshop, bookshop and restaurant. The ruins of the mill in the Howk have a wheel pit, which demonstrates the enormous size of the waterwheel on this site.

The Howk is a lovely little glen-like valley, with water rushing over the limestone in a series of rapids and falls. The village has been designated as a Conservation Area.

The Walk

Leave the car park by the vehicular exit, up to the road by the exten-

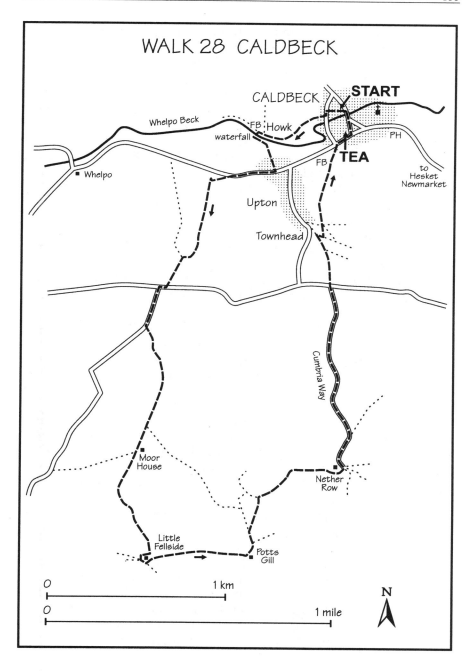

WALK 28 CALDBECK

CALDBECK

START

Whelpo Beck

FB · Howk

waterfall

Whelpo

FB

TEA

PH

to
Hesket
Newmarket

Upton

Townhead

Cumbria Way

Moor
House

Nether
Row

Little
Fellside

Potts
Gill

0   1 km

0   1 mile

N

sive village green. Turn left and then right in 40m between farm buildings, at a sign 'footpath to Howk'. Go along a broad track to a kissing gate and continue, soon reaching the ruins of the old mill, with its immense wheel pit.

Carry on up the steps beside the rushing beck, cross the footbridge and go up to a kissing gate. Turn left to follow the field boundary, keep right of farm buildings and go through another kissing gate to join a public road.

Turn right. Pass a few dwellings, including Davaar House, then turn left at a signposted farm gate. Take the faintly worn path over grass, rising by a line of trees and bending left, uphill, following a shallow depression. Continue through a gate/stile, along a track bounded by old hedges.

As this track appears to terminate, go left for a few metres to an ar-rowed post and continue uphill, now with a hedge on the right. There are good views over Caldbeck village. On reaching a cross wall look carefully for a stile over the wall on the right. Go over and keep the same line, now with the wall on the left, to a stile giving ac-cess to a minor road.

Turn right, then left in 30m at a junction, signposted 'Fellside and Branthwaite'. In about 200m turn left at a gate/stile to follow a path which soon converges with a wall on the left. After a stile stay beside a fence on the left. Ahead are the well rounded shapes of the Cald-beck Fells.

After further gates/stiles the ruin of Moor House is approached and the barely visible path cuts across between clumps of rushes. Beyond the ruin go over a ladder stile and follow a terrace across a small field, ignoring a stile on the right. Go over a stile ahead and de-scend to cross a small beck by a farm vehicle bridge.

Ascend the opposite hillside along a depression in the ground to a gate/stile in the top left corner of the field. Go through Little Fellside Farm, turning right at a concrete roadway to pass in front of the farm. Go over a cattle grid and turn left over close cropped grass, close to a boundary wall.

Keep the wall close on the left for about 200m from the farm to find a well concealed stile. Look over the wall, pass a small field and, 25m beyond the cross wall, the stile is found behind a growth of rushes. Go over and turn right to walk over short grass, in line with the wall. As Potts Gill (farm) is approached, go over a stile and across a garden-like area with small trees to another part concealed stile over a stone wall, close to a dwelling. Go over, pass between buildings and through a farm gate, then turn left down the farm access roadway.

Stay with this roadway, bearing right and dipping to cross a beck, Blea Wath, before reaching Nether Row. At a junction of several farm access roadways turn left along a surfaced road, part of the Cumbria Way. The grass verge provides good walking for about three-quarters of a mile.

At a junction go straight ahead into a rough, narrow, lane. Just before reaching the outlying buildings of Townhead turn right for a few metres over grass at a 'Cumbria Way' signpost to a stile with a yellow waymark. Cross a small field, keeping to the right of Townhead and ignoring the prominent farm gate, to go over a stile. Cross a lane to go over another stile. Continue with a fence/hedge on the left, enter sparse woodland over a stile and descend to a footbridge, passing a former millpond on the left.

Go along a narrow track between fences. On the right is a former mill site, with a rather incongruous reconstructed mill wheel, then a modern residential area. At the public road turn right; the tea shop is at the first road junction, on the left. The public conveniences are on the right, by the clog maker's workshop.

After refreshment turn left, cross the Cald Beck, and turn left into the car park.

29. Pooley Bridge and Ullswater

Length: 6¼ miles (a little less if a short cut is used)

Summary: A fine circuit over the high ground to the south-east of Ullswater, with the return to Pooley Bridge using the lake shore path. Some uphill walking but, as the highest point is only 320m (1050ft), this is not excessive and there are no steep gradients. Good paths, mainly grassy, with just a little mud as the only possible difficulty.

Car Parking: Public car park in Pooley Bridge (pay and display in season). Grid reference 471244.

Map: Ordnance Survey Outdoor Leisure no. 5, The English Lakes, north-eastern area, 1:25,000 or Landranger no. 90, Penrith and Keswick, 1:50,000.

Tea Shop

At Tree Tops Café everything on the menu is available all day; so it is even possible to start with some of the breakfast goodies before the walk. Cooked to order, there is a combination of just about everything one might wish to eat for breakfast or maybe one might just settle for a bacon sandwich. Imaginatively, there is also a cooked vegetarian breakfast. For later in the day, or for the more health conscious, omelettes and salads are popular too. The Lake District cream tea includes a sandwich, scone with jam and cream – or for high tea, home cooked fish and chips is tempting following the walk. Children's meals are available. Prices very reasonable. Tree Tops is a clean, busy café with friendly counter service right in the centre of Pooley Bridge village.

Open: 9am to 6pm summer and 10am to 4pm winter every day but weekends only in November and December and closed all January. Tel: 017684 86267

About the Area

Although not one of Lakeland's major honeypots, Pooley Bridge is a pleasant little place, strategically situated at the foot of Ullswater, by the terminus of the seasonal lake 'steamer' service to and from Glenridding and Howtown. The village can become busy in season; to cater for present day needs there are two inns, a few shops including two tea shops, and public conveniences.

For about one square mile the moorland at Moor Divock, between Pooley Bridge and Askham/Helton has a late Neolithic/early bronze age ritual landscape, with field clearance cairns overlying features such as the stone circle at the 'Cockpit', very close to the line of this walk. Much later came the Romans, driving their 'High Street' over the top of the mountain which bears this name. The line of this road passes Moor Divock on its way towards Penrith.

In more modern times William and Dorothy Wordsworth were frequent visitors to their friends the Clarksons, who lived at the dignified house Eusemere which occupies a superb position facing up Ullswater. The house is very evident towards the end of this walk.

Laid up for winter: "raven" near Pooley Bridge

The Walk

Turn right from the car park to walk through Pooley Bridge village, with a preview of the Tree Tops tea shop. At the road junction by St Paul's church turn right along the road signposted to Howtown and Martindale. At the next road junction go straight across into a cul de sac road, gently uphill.

Pass a caravan site entrance and then Roehead Farm. At a gate with a 'public bridleway Helton' sign the road loses its surface to continue as a broad easy track across open hillside, the flank of

WALK 29 POOLEY BRIDGE AND ULLSWATER

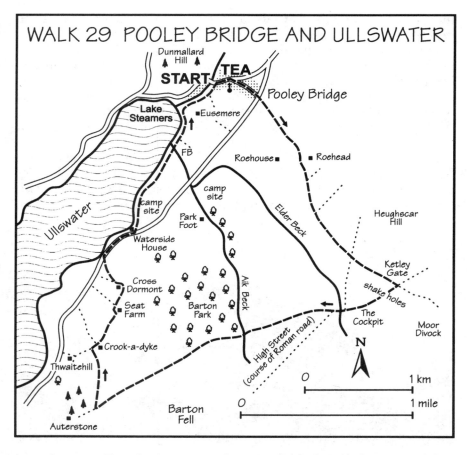

Heughscar Hill and a favourite place for skylarks. At the crest of this track is a major cross paths, with signpost. Turn right here.

To cut the corner turn right at a more minor cross paths about a third of a mile before the crest to take a narrow but obvious path. Cross a beck and stay with the path as it goes to the right initially before bearing left to aim for the top edge of Barton Park plantation, where it joins the major track. Or, turn left 30m after the beck to follow the Ordnance Survey right of way along rather less obvious paths to join the major path near the 'Cockpit'. If using either of these short cuts, turn right on joining the major path.

On the major path fork right at a cairn and continue to Aik Beck, crossed at the near edge of the plantation. Keep right to reach a 'Howtown 2¾' signpost. The views up the lake are improving all the time; a wonderful scene including Helvellyn and its outliers, with the closer Place Fell dominant.

After passing the plantation a lovely grassy track descends gently downhill, every bit as attractive as the celebrated Loughrigg Terrace at Grasmere, but without the crowds. At the near end of Auterstone Wood turn very sharp right at a 'Pooley Bridge' sign to follow a lesser footpath over grass, marked by white topped posts along the way, along the side of a diffuse stream, then between clumps of gorse.

Go through a kissing gate to join a farm driveway, turning right. There is a 'Pooley Bridge' sign on the back of the wall. To the left is Thwaites Hill Farm. Pass Crook-a-dyke farm and go over grass to a gate with yellow arrow waymark then along the edge of a field to a stile and on to Seat Farm, passed through the gate on the left. Cross the access roadway to a little gate signposted 'footpath Cross Dormont' After a signposted stile go diagonally left across a field to another stile by Cross Dormont Farm, which has a prominent bank barn. Reach the access road below the farm, turn left for 100m, then turn right, over a stile. Angle left across a pathless field, pass two marker posts, and join the public road at a kissing gate.

Turn right for approximately⅓ mile to reach Waterside House, a working farm and caravan/camping site. Turn left here between the buildings at a 'footpath Pooley Bridge' sign and then turn right to follow the lake shore path back to Pooley Bridge, an entirely uncomplicated delightful waterside stroll, helped by a boardwalk across wet ground. As the village is approached, Eusemere can be seen on the right, then the eponymous bridge on the left.

Should you want to return to your vehicle before visiting the tea shop, a small gate gives direct access to the car park.

30. Glenridding and Lanty's Tarn

Length: 4½ miles

Summary: A generally easy walk in the Glenridding valley, with a short but steep ascent to Lanty's Tarn at the outset. No difficulties underfoot.

Car Parking: Main pay and display car park at Glenridding village. Grid reference 387170.

Map: Ordnance Survey Outdoor Leisure no. 5, The English Lakes, north-eastern area, 1:25,000 or Landranger no. 90, Penrith and Keswick, 1:50,000.

Tea Shop

Newly opened in 1997 Kilners Coffee Shop at The Glenridding Hotel is smart, shiny clean, and inviting. The room is large with attractive furniture and on a cold wet day was warm and welcoming. Orders for food are taken at the self-select counter and then brought across to the table. Hot dishes are available each day and there is always a cauldron of soup, jacket potatoes with a choice of fillings, highly recommended bacon sandwiches, scones, cakes etc. Drinks include good quality coffee and tea, milk shakes, and various cold drinks. Although under the same ownership as the hotel, the coffee shop is in a separate building. Being a new enterprise, the menu and hours may be varied.

Open: Mid-February to end of October 10am to 5pm every day. Other months open only on Saturdays and Sundays. Tel: 017684 82228

About the Area

Glenridding is a former mining village by the shore of Ullswater, with a main street running up the valley of the same name towards the former Greenside lead mine which, until its closure in 1962, played an important part in providing local employment. For such a small place, Glenridding is well provided with shops and has two fair sized hotels.

The very important mine was in virtually continuous use from the middle of the 17th century and no less than 50 of the houses in Glen-

Ullswater "steamer" at Glenridding

ridding are late Victorian former mine cottages. Large scale modernisation of the mine in the late 19th century included the use of the first electric mine locomotive in Britain. In 1927 a dam high up the valley burst during a storm, resulting in a flood, which swept through the village, causing great damage but fortunately no loss of life. A headland pushing out into the lake close to the steamer pier remains as evidence of this disaster.

Keldas, close to Lanty's Tarn, is a very minor peak which can be visited as a short diversion from the basic route of this walk. It is noteworthy as the viewpoint for the classic view along Ullswater.

Patterdale is an attractive hamlet a mile or so south of Glenridding on the road to the Kirkstone Pass and Windermere. **St Patrick's Well** is by the roadside, on the right, almost opposite a little marina with snack hut.

In the opinion of many, Ullswater is the most beautiful of the English Lakes, its three reaches encompassing most of the landscape variation which makes the district so uniquely beautiful. To travel on the lake 'steamers', particularly towards the head of the lake, is sheer delight.

The Walk

Leave the car park by the main entrance, turn right, cross Glenridding Beck on the road bridge, and turn right again to walk along the roadway past the front of a row of shops, with the beck now on the right.

The road soon loses its surface, becoming a rising, broad, stony track. As the track forks, keep left, uphill, following a signpost ' Lanty's Tarn, Helvellyn'. Close to a few cottages there are two waymarks. Keep right here. Turn left over a little footbridge and go through a gate before climbing steeply uphill Go through a kissing gate with signpost, the path now rising more gently before turning sharp left, close to another kissing gate. Follow the signpost 'Striding Edge and Grisedale'.

There are views to the left over Ullswater before the woodland which surrounds the delightful Lanty's Tarn is reached, through a gate. The diversion to the top of Keldas goes up to the left before the gate.

For views over Grisedale to St Sunday Crag, walk a little beyond the far end of the tarn. On a raw December day a pair of Goldeneye

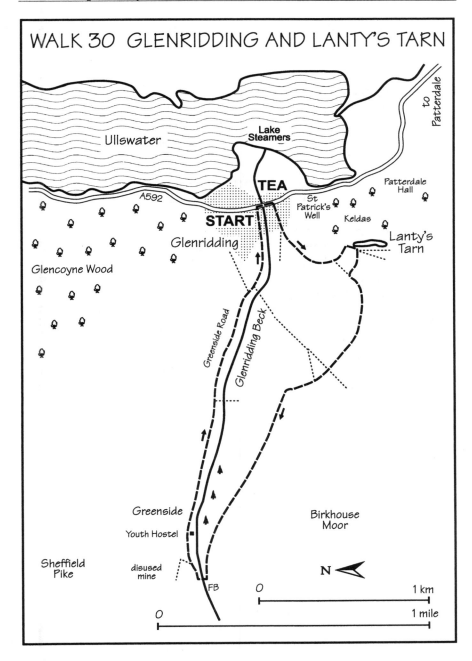

WALK 30 GLENRIDDING AND LANTY'S TARN

to Patterdale

Ullswater

Lake Steamers

TEA

A592

START

St Patrick's Well

Patterdale Hall

Glenridding

Keldas

Lanty's Tarn

Glencoyne Wood

Greenside Road

Glenridding Beck

Greenside

Youth Hostel

Birkhouse Moor

Sheffield Pike

disused mine

N

FB

0

1 km

0

1 mile

ducks paddled around, seemingly quite oblivious to the blustery weather.

To continue, return to the kissing gate and then turn left at once to take a barely worn path along the side of the wall. At a cross wall there is a ladder stile or a gated way through sheep pens for the less agile. After the sheep pens, stay with the wall as far as a gate on the left which brings a more used path from Grisedale.

Turn right to follow this grassy track through rushes, bending left to terrace across the hillside, with more views of Ullswater and Place Fell, with Sheffield Pike across the valley. An engineered portion of path drops to cross Mires Beck. After the beck another path from the valley bottom joins on the right and the track, now downhill, is more obviously well used.

At a junction keep right, close to a wall, heading for the obvious scarred site of the former Greenside lead mine. At another fork keep right, still by the wall. Join a more important looking path and bend left, with the ravine of the Glenridding Beck below on the right. Pass a dam with a sluice and fork right to cross the footbridge. From this area the shapely peak visible up the valley is Catstye Cam. Turn right to follow the old mine roadway down to the remaining buildings, converted to leisure uses, including a youth hostel.

The mine access road, Greenside Road, now provides an easy and unmistakable route back to Glenridding. Follow the village street to the main road and the car park. The teashop is found at the prominent Glenridding Hotel.

Tea Shop Walks – Spreading everywhere!

The Sigma Leisure Tea Shop Walks series already includes:

Cheshire
The Chilterns
The Cotswolds
The Lake District, Volume 1
The Lake District, Volume 2
Lancashire
Leicestershire & Rutland
North Devon
The Peak District
Shropshire
Snowdonia
South Devon
Staffordshire
Surrey & Sussex
Warwickshire
The Yorkshire Dales

Each book costs £6.95 and contains an average of 25 excellent walks: far better value than any other competitor!

In case of difficulty, or for a free catalogue, please contact:
SIGMA LEISURE,
1 SOUTH OAK LANE, WILMSLOW, CHESHIRE SK9 6AR.
Phone: 01625-531035;
Fax: 01625-536800.
E-mail: sigma.press@zetnet.co.uk .
Web site: http//www.sigmapress.co.uk

VISA and MASTERCARD orders welcome. Please add £2 p&p to all orders.

Tea is our most social and
sociable drink – a part of our
national heritage and daily life for
well over 300 years. The Tea Club
exists so its members can share
and enjoy the history, traditions
and romance associated with this
fascinating drink.

 **MAGAZINE**

 **EVENTS**

 **COMPETITIONS**

 **MEMBER DISCOUNTS**

 **TASTINGS & SAMPLING**

 **A FREE GIFT WHEN
YOU JOIN**

THERE'S SO MUCH MORE

TO TEA THAN JUST

A CUPPA !

HOW TO JOIN

Simply send your name, full address and postcode to:

The Tea Club

PO Box 221

Guildford, Surrey GU1 3YT

and an application form will be sent to you immediately.

Tea Club Memberships are also a great gift idea – why not send one to a friend !

TSW/1